WENCE

NOSTRADAMUS DECODED

CRUX EDITION

OTHER BOOKS BY THE AUTHOR:

ANCIENT ECOLOGISTS	(an e-book and a pb)
SKY GODS & ANGELS	(an e-book and a pb)

Or Our Ancestors Return From Space to Earth

Revised version
Cover art by Jock Hildebrand

Published by
Earth Way Society
306-1349 Bertram Street
Kelowna, B.C. V1Y 8N4
Canada

ISBN 978-0-9916741-6-9 (e-book)
ISBN 978-0-9916741-5-2 (paperback)

CONTENTS

INTRODUCTION

Nostradamus' prophecies are like a 4-D puzzle. Their stories are coded in the language of ancient myths, and the time references, where inserted deliberately, are inaccurate, and only my failure and subsequent re-readings enabled me to narrow down the range within which the key event, namely the asteroid impact, is to take place, that will trigger the subsequent events, described by the seer in such incredible details.

Of course, their accuracy still remains to be ascertained, but their enormous extent, which includes some 600 quatrains, out of less than 1,000, covering decades of the 21st century, is just impossible to comprehend – if they were to be accepted as an achievement of a mere mortal, which they are not.

To start with, astrologers of Nostradamus' era claimed his skills were very average at that art. But even if he were an exceptionally good astrologer, there is simply no way such predictions can ever be made with the help of relevant charts, by staring into a crystal ball or a bowl of water, as some people claim.

Furthermore, the seer made no secret of the fact these predictions were indeed intended mainly for the coming decades of our time period, to be launched by an asteroid impact, as he clearly states in his enigmatic Letter to King Henry II of France: "Most of the events … described (are) going … to the events which will take place at the beginning of the seventh millenary." This, the seventh millennium from the alleged creation of the world, according to the Bible and the relevant scholars, started in 2005 CE. But that was the second closest he got with his dating, because, without realizing it, he also indicated in one of his quatrains that the train of events will start after 2014.

There were other attempts made at dating this key event in

human existence, and while they all failed with a varying degree of inaccuracy, most of them plainly point to our era. The Mayas got the closest, choosing the date 12.21.12. The next nearest one was the Babylonian astronomer / priest Berossus, who arrived at the date 5.5.2000. Nostradamus, very reluctantly and with great reservation, chose August 1999, most likely because he knew a solar eclipse was to take place over Europe at that time, and the appearance of the fateful asteroid is to coincide with one. The Indian priests of Kali pegged the period down to the middle of the 19th century, which triggered the Indian uprising. Jesus was off by whopping 2,000 years, when he promised essentially the same event was to take place during the lifetime of his disciples.

There are other predictions that also suggest this momentous event will take place during our era. For example, according to the line-up of popes, foretold, so far correctly, by Saint Malachi, some 900 years ago, Pope Francis is likely the last Pope, who "will tend his sheep amidst numerous tribulations. These having passed, (Rome) will be destroyed." And Nostradamus provides details of the circumstances, connected directly to the asteroid's impact.

Another clergyman, Johann Friede, (1204-1257), was more to the point. He predicted: "When the great time will come, in which mankind will face its last, hard trial, it will be foreshadowed by striking changes in nature. Not all of it will be the result of natural causes (as) mankind will gamble with its own existence. Before the powers of destruction will succeed … the world will be thrown into disorder and the age of iron will plunge into nothingness."

If it needs pointing out, this rather modern sounding statement perfectly fits our times, for its obvious climatic warning, and because, since antiquity till now, the historical period has been known as the Age of Iron – metal we are soon to run out of anyhow.

Even some ancient Greek writers, like Homer, or playwrights, like Aeschylus, along with some Roman poets, such as Virgil, got into the 'business' of prophecies, as we shall see. Yet, none of them had claimed to be a prophet. They 'merely' echoed knowledge, then wide-spread among the educated population; knowledge fairly liberally disseminated through the Eleusinian mysteries school in Greece, and by the so called Roman Sibyls, located outside Naples. It is said of the Roman Sibyls that they used to posses nine books of prophecies, one for each of the last nine millenniums. Of these, I am convinced, a copy of the last one did somehow survive and came into Nostradamus' hands, while on the lam from Inquisition in Italy, which he later reshaped into 'his' prophecies.

Another indicator pointing in the same direction is the tradition of Saturnalia, first celebrated in Persia, some 3,500 years ago, and centuries later in Rome, around the time of the winter equinox, but also in India, Mesopotamia, even among the Mayas and the Incas, and until about 5,000 years ago likely also in Egypt. And, interestingly enough, without realizing it, again, one of the seer's quatrains indicates the event is to take place in December, also around the time of winter equinox.

At the heart of the Saturnalia were utopian aspects of joyful carelessness and perfect peace, along with disquieting elements of threat and danger. Yet, all of these values fit the rather detailed description of the coming Age of Saturn, which Nostradamus talks about repeatedly.

While in China Saturnalia celebration was unknown, the ancient Chinese, contrarily to intuition, used to consider summer the season of death and winter the season of renewal and life. And curiously enough, the Persian myth of Ahura Mazda, the God of Light and Life, helps to explain why.

Tradition claims this myth is, by now, some 12,000 years old, and it asserts that, back then, "evil entered the world," in form of an entity known as Ahriman, who essentially replaced Ahura Mazda, but he is to return in the 12,000 years time to resume his reign.

To understand what really took place, those long millennia ago, we have to turn to climatology for our answer, to the detrimental effect extreme climatic change has on humans.

By now the climatologists know, but prefer not to talk about the fact, that some 11,700 years ago the global temperature shot up by at least 10C, in the wake of the post-Ice-Age apocalyptic upheavals, above the 20th century global average of 15C. This, in turn, is confirmed by a Hittite myth of The Vanished God, which claims that forests and springs dried up, that humans and other mammals lost the ability to procreate. But this could happen only if the global temperature average had exceeded 24C, as the Greenland's ice cores suggest actually did happen.

Humans obviously survived, in the northern polar regions, but in the process had lost almost 20 percent of their brains, by volume, and about 50 percent of their neural connections, again confirmed, in a symbolic fashion, by a variety of myths. This transformation horrified people who, for long millennia, kept reminding themselves of the fact by stories in which they saw themselves as being "asleep," or being "living dead," or as living in prison.

But the most serious deficiency people had suffered from was the loss of their ability to receive communication from the God. No, not Yahweh, but the Cosmic Being, aka the Universe, known to quantum physicists, who claim, to a great displeasure of other scientists, that this Being knew the entire future even before the Universe got started. In fact this Being had to be Omniscient, in order to overcome all the otherwise inexplicable mathematical impossibilities associated with the formation and organization of the physical universe, and later on of life, on planets like Earth.

What these material scientists do not, and cannot, explain either, is the presence of quantum computers inside each living cell, known as microtubules, which also provide support structure and transport system for cells. And it was through these quantum computers in human brains the Cosmic Being used to communicate useful information to our forebears, before their critical mass collapsed, via quantum magnetism, in existence since the so called Big Bang, as the latest research confirms.

A key part of the information, transmitted about 12,000 years ago, when people still had the capacity to receive it, were the details of mankind's fate during the millennia of this peculiar "inter-regnum." Yet, since the first 2,000 years of it were a virtual non-existence, as mankind was reduced to a number of tribes, surviving on a primitive level, and it took over 1,000 years for their numbers to recoup enough for them to start forming new civilizations, these predictions, as we shall see, concerned themselves only with the subsequent nine millennia.

It is also from these prophecies, which in their presumed entirety remained only with the Roman Sibyls, but used to be once known literally all around the world, that all the major prophecies were derived from, including those found in the Bible. After all, as it says even there, only God knows the future. And it also assures the readers that in the Kingdom of God, identical with the return of Saturn, men and women will again be able to "prophecy," that is to receive communication from the Cosmic Being, which subject Nostradamus gets into in a much greater detail.

The assertion that only the Cosmic Being knows the future applies, as indicated, to Nostradamus as well. Yet, to accuse him of plagiarism would be grossly unfair, as he most likely merely performed a predestined service to mankind and the Cosmic Being, which, in the view of the classical Greeks, would make him a "hero," for they believed that every person chosen by the goddess Hera, a yet another personification of Gaia, or Mother Earth, as well as of the Cosmic Being, to serve her purposes. The most famous of these is Hercules who, being nominally responsible for transforming the seat of the formative culture from one place and one set of peoples to another, and other tasks associated with maintaining civilization, was, as a sign of honour, given the goddess very name, which he then carried for millennia,

By preserving this hoary prophecy Nostradamus also preserved hope for mankind, especially on the North American continent, to where this abstract Hercules is now transferring the seat of the formative culture from Europe, while he also indicated that a major social change will take place on the continent in the near future, to complete the transformation of the local culture.

Furthermore, by making it plain that all the (near) future events have been orchestrated by the Cosmic Being, the seer is helping to renew the awareness of this Entity, of Its direct involvement in mankind's existence.

Also, considering the wealth of phrophecies listed above, along with the accurate description of the current situation in the United States and of its formative stages, it is all but impossible to suggest they are all "lucky guesses" on the seer's part, including the predictions of current technology and climatic changes. The same applies to the reversal of the current situation, whose importance was deemed so vital that its memory was kept alive in Europe not only till the medieval times, but right to the period of the French Revolution.

For example, a series of allegorical engravings, done by the German artist H.S. Beham, who was Nostradamus' contemporary, portray the current Age of Jupiter as frivolous and self-indulgent, and the coming Age of Saturn as a bucolic one, living contently close to nature, just as it was also portrayed by Thomas More, at roughly the same time, in his Utopia.

In his Letter to Henry II Nostradamus also stated two further predictions: 1. That during the time of the French Revolution people "will believe (it) to be the period, the epoch of renewal," which was a wrong assumption. It was also reported that someone left the book of Nostradamus' prophecies open in Paris, on the very page of this prediction. 2. His message for our times, concerning his prophecies, stated that "the memory of things contained in such instruments will suffer incalculable loss ..."

The "instruments" are not only the predictions themselves, but also the keys to their understanding. The most blatant difference can be seen in the expectations associated with such predictions. As noted, till the 18th century people were expecting a "re-birth," or the "return of the ages," whereas nowadays such expectations are almost exclusively associated with a wholesale destruction. While both are bound to take place, in stages, the positive aspects of this evolutionary process have been erased from the communal mind, as we have forgotten the true meaning of myths, of the key words of the ancient language that spelled it out, and which Nostradamus was still acquainted with.

Unfortunately, myths started to suffer from misunderstanding since the times of the classical Greeks, as they themselves no longer understood the ancient language that gives their gods, but mainly their goddesses, their true meaning, and thus also the meaning to their myths. Yet, in China, of roughly the same period, myths were virtually outlawed, as they were deemed to portray events, places and characters that did not exist. In modern times, thanks to Darwinism, which heavily favours an express evolution of human species, suddenly taking off about 6,000 years ago, science inflicted further indecency upon myths, interpreting these "psychologically," usually resorting to Freud's sexed-up method, instead of using the ecological, evolutionary and scientific perspective they demand. Sadly, the study of myths themselves ceased to exist in North America, since no university, it would seem, offers such a study. Thus the "incalculable loss ..."

It then should come as no surprise that most of interpretations of the seer's quatrains were done from the perspective of astrology, or simply conjured up out of thin air, to please the contemporary crowd, in spite the explicit warning against such attempts.

"May those who read this verse think upon it deeply.
Let the profane and ignorant herd keep away.
Let all astrologers, simpletons and barbarians stay far off.
He who does otherwise, let him be the priest of the rite." 6/100

Here the word "rite" refers to the prescribed form of words, expressions and images, as used since ancient times, and replicated by Nostradamus in his quatrains, which, to repeat myself, can be gleaned only from a proper understanding of the ancient myth, which he also refers to, even directly quotes from.

Lacking the understanding our ancestors took for granted, these would be interpreters frequently marked his quatrains as "occult," when they were merely beyond their limited understanding.

Yet, today the frontiers of the New Sciences, whether in quantum mechanics or in microbiology, are currently also beyond human understanding, as the top scientists readily acknowledge:

"The generative order enfolds orders that go beyond those that can be contained even in the quantum domain, orders that have been so far 'hidden' to science." David Bohm

"Molecule seemed like a little machine ... but during the last few years it grew almost impossibly complex ... beyond the current understanding." Lewis Thomas

These two examples illustrate that even the New Sciences have their "hidden" or "occult" dimension, which cannot be understood, but certain aspects of it can be grasped by the human mind and such a comprehension, even if limited, can be used, and is being used, for "scientific predictions," better known as "theories." In this respect, Nostradamus', and other such predictions, are not all that dissimilar from the scientific ones.

The same, though, applies to the so called "occult" quatrains, whose understanding can be acquired by trawling through all kinds of relevant books, with a publication date of at least circa twenty years ago, or more, available practically from every library, provided the person has the curiosity necessary to inquire a bit more deeply into the reality of this world, which, ultimately, is what this book offers.

SUN AGE, MOON AGE, AND OTHER SYMBOLS

This chapter, along with many others, is so complex, it is virtually impossible to arrange the quatrains within them in a chronological order. We should also keep in mind that Nostradamus, as noted, was employing in his prophecies an ancient lore whose vestiges have survived among the initiates till about the 17th century. And it is the meanings of this ancient lore we will be discussing here.

A part of the key is hidden in the seer's family surname, adopted by his great-grandfather on his paternal side, a royal physician, who most likely also had access to the sources of ancient wisdom. He chose the name Nostradamus, which translates "Of Our Lady." Seeing this name the first idea that would come to most people's mind is that it refers to Mary, the Mother of Jesus. It very well might, but it most likely contained a double meaning, known only to people acquainted with hermetic knowledge, which the Jews of southern France, from whom Nostradamus descended, certainly were. The fact of the matter is that the honorific "Lady" is of a much older vintage, than the one associated with Christianity. Many of the ancient goddesses, such as Hera, Leda, or Astarte used to be known as a "Lady." The same honorific also used to be bestowed upon many an ancient "mother of gods," or of a god, which was nominally also the case of Mary, known as Saint Mary.

Even the name Mary, either as the Mother of Jesus, or as Mary Magdalene, did not "sneak" into the Christian lore by an accident. The name Mary, Mari, Mare, refers to the most ancient of the goddesses, to the goddess of the seas, of whom we shall talk a bit more later on, because the seer mentions the revival of her religion.

One of the other ancient goddesses to whom Nostradamus, directly or indirectly, refers to more than once, used to be also known as "The Mistress," albeit as the "Mistress of the Wild Beasts." Her name was, and is, Artemis. Strangely enough, even her composite name, "Ar-temis," is made up of a (she) bear prefix, the "Ar," while the suffix, "Temis," again refers to the same most ancient sea goddess known to the Greeks as Themis. As such, Artemis also used to be known as the patron goddess of sailors.

Her "beasts," on closer examination, which we cannot go into at this stage, represent various human qualities, and / or totemic clans, known as bears, wolfs, horses, etc. Furthermore, the honorific "Mistress" can be easily transposed for "The Lady," who, after all, is the Mistress of her house. To be more specific, as was understood in the ancient days, her "house" is the planet, and in turn the "house" is herself. Yes, we are talking about the planet, personified as Gaia, besides many other names.

Perhaps the most convincing argument that Nostradamus did not deem himself named after the Mother of Jesus is the incident recorded by the authorities in Agen, where he at one time lived. He remarked to a workman, casting a bronze statue of the Virgin, that he was making devils or, as we would say today, casting heathen images. The Inquisition was then after him for heresy, and he had to flee for his life.

Perhaps this much will suffice to establish the fact that the seer was extensively employing imagery we today associate with "myths," but which in fact is a part of an ancient system of knowledge, and the organizational system of this knowledge that, among other things, understood the climatic and evolutionary cycles, and their intimate relationship, which is currently being rediscovered by some contemporary scientists. In the last line of quatrain 10/41 he explicitly states about himself that he lived "surrounded by sleepwalkers & the great myth."

I also need to point out here one other important aspect of Nostradamus' predictions, before we start interpreting them; namely the fact that the vast majority of seemingly astrological references are in fact references to various evolutionary cycles, or ages, of a fairly recent past, designated in historical times by the names of metals and their perceived value. That is the Golden Age, the Silver Age, the Bronze Age, and the Iron Age. Each of these Ages in turn had its ruling deity, known as Uranus, Cronus, Zeus and Dionysus to the Greeks. Nostradamus though had decided to simplify this system, or perhaps followed a more ancient pattern, that limited the cosmic influences to just two polarities: the good and the evil. As a result he opted for two major deities, Cronus and Zeus, while referring to them by their better known Roman names, Saturn and Jupiter, which also happen to be the names of planets, and this then seriously waylaid his astrological 'interpreters'.

At the same time, just to keep us on our mental toes, the seer had also designated Saturn as the Age of the Sun, and Jupiter as the Age of the Moon, whose existence so baffled the astrologers so badly, their guesstimates for its reign ranged from a few years to a full 1,000 years, but is none of those. Also, almost every time he mentions the name of Mercury, he refers to the perceived alchemical properties of this metal as a transformative agent – albeit on the scale of human societies, not as a planet on an astrological chart.

It should also be pointed out that the Golden Age is a synonym for the Age of the Sun, by which is meant the period of time when the inner light of mankind's mental and spiritual energies shone with their full force. The Silver, Bronze, and the Iron Ages are all synonymous with the Age of the Moon, the period of time which represents the "night," and the mental sleep of mankind, during which its inner light is obscured, and shines only dimly, with a borrowed light, like the Moon. (The "borrowed" light usually comes from the subconscious.) As such this Age started those circa 11,700 years ago and continues till the present time.

It might be of more than passing interest to note here that the alchemists used to symbolize Saturn's (Cronus') motive power by dragons, while dragons, pythons, dolphins, etc., symbolize the ice age glaciers in mythological systems. Also, Saturn's designated element used to be the earth. (And earthiness.) However, we also know from the Greek mythology, Cronus used to be known for devouring his children. In the coming period this fact will again come to pass, and the myth, once more, will become reality. Jupiter's motive power used to be symbolized by peacocks, and his element was designated as power and vanity—which so perfectly fits the passing era.

There are also other cycles, measuring and dividing the time, but for the sake of clarity we will discuss these in the chapter titled Time Cycles and Converging Prophecies. Here we shall concentrate predominantly on the Age of the Sun and the Age of the Moon.

As we will also see, to complicate the situation even further,

Nostradamus sometimes associates the symbolical meanings assigned to various planets, as well as the Sun and the Moon, to the various conflicting parties of the future.

In other words, the seer's prophecies are a real complex puzzle, each piece consisting of wheels within wheels, and these in turn placed inside each other like a set of Russian dolls.

For example, in quatrain 9/44 we read: "Saturn will change from gold to iron. Those against it will be exterminated ..." On the surface, these two short sentences appear to be merely a dark gibberish, especially if we were to take the Saturn named here for the planet. But we already know it is the Age of Saturn that is implied, which in turn is the synonym for the future Age of the Sun, that will, at the moment of its inauguration, change 'temporarily' back into the destructive Iron Age, that is, into a war.

Having established the validity of the interpretative key makes it also much easier to decipher the otherwise almost undecipherable anagrams as well. For example, we can claim with greater conviction that the name of Raypoz is an anagram (Zapory) for Saturn. Another anagram for Saturn appears in quatrain 6/70: "The Great Chyren will boss the world ... He will be greatly satisfied with the sole title of the victor." The context reveals this quatrain is about Saturn, and even the name, when rearranged as Ceyhrn, sounds, when spoken, almost as Saturn.

In quatrain 3/92 we read: "The world is near its final period. Saturn will again be late on his return." Since the planet Saturn returns with a clockwork precision every 29.5 years, and since, obviously, no discrepancy had been noticed by astronomers in its orbit or periodicity, the seer, again, meant the Age of Saturn. Then, in quatrain 5/87, he states: "In the year that Saturn is freed from servitude, the Frankish territory will be inundated by water." This, as we shall see later, ties this prediction to the one contained in quatrain 9/44, mentioned above.

Throughout the relevant quatrains the master will treat us to sentences such as: "The tyrant Selim will be put to death at a harbour ..."(1/94), when referring to the Age of the Moon, and to Latin and Greek word for Moon, "Selen," or he will say: "When all is well, all Solary and Lunary well ..." while referring to the blend of the solar and lunar qualities of the current Western civilization, its "balance" of conscious and subconscious drives. And these are the relatively easy ones. Then we have quatrains like the one numbered 5/53:

"The Law of the Sun contending with Venus,
approaching the spirit of prophecy:
Neither the one nor the other are understood.
The Law of the Great Messiah retained throughout the Sun."

As will be explained in greater detail in chapter "New Culture for Old," "The Law of the Sun" represents here the American, i.e. the U.S. culture and foreign policy, contending with that of Europe, represented here by Venus. But to explain why Nostradamus chose Venus to represent Europe will require a rather lengthy explanation.

To start with, it has nothing to do with the qualities of this goddess, who is related to Aphrodite and many other ancient goddesses, but strictly to her name, whose origin, the historians claim, is obscure.

While her name does not appear in Italy until the first millennium B.C.E., we have to look for her origin, 'surprisingly', to central Europe. An ancient nation / tribe used to reside there, from which all the European, and most likely all the Indo-European people and languages have sprung. These people became historically known as the Wends. Their key goddess was named Lubus, whose name is still retained in name places, such as Lubock in Germany, or Lubljana in Slovenia, and others. It could be translated as "the words of love," but its meaning most likely represented Logos, the source of world order and intelligibility. As a noun this word is related also to the word "lip," and this brings to mind the name of the Hindu goddess Vac, whose name meant "mouth," and who was known as the Mother of the Vedas, or we might say the Mother of Knowledge, which goes right back to the concept of the Logos. That very name seems directly related to Lubus as well, by a linguistic descent. (As in Logos, Lobos, Lubus, or vice a versa.)

The leading core element of the Wends migrated to northern Italy, around the middle of the first millennium B.C.E., where they became known as the Veneti. The name Venus then came into existence by combining their name, VENds, with that of their native goddess lubUS, resulting in VENUS, again a sea goddess by nature, but one who, because of her original character, was still being referred to as the "Goddess of Love." The other name she was known by to the Romans was Libitina, which still echoes her native one. Furthermore, in the original Indo-European language "wen-es" meant "love," and "leubh" also meant "love," as well as "desire," or "to care." The root word "wen," by itself also meant "desire." It would not take too much imagination either to transpose the letter "e" for "u", in the Indo-European word Wen-es, (love), to end up with Wen-us.

Since Nostradamus, as would seem obvious, understood the genealogy of European nations, his idea to refer to them, symbolically, as "Venus" was an ingenious shorthand, whose meaning became virtually obliterated by time. At the same time though, because the same Veneti also founded the city of Venice, (Venezia in Italian), which later became the capital of a commercial empire, Nostradamus sometimes also uses the word Venus to symbolize commerce as well, or Venetians to designate Europeans.

The seer's message must become even murkier for the readers and the interpreters when they come across quatrains like the one numbered 9/74:

> "In the homicidal city of Fertsod,
> again & again many oxen plough, not sacrificed.
> A repeated return to the honors of Artemis,
> and to Vulcan to bury the dead."

Because of the reference to Artemis, I would assume the "city" of Fertsod is pointing in the direction of a multiple, but overlapping choice: to ferrous, or iron and weapons, thus homicide, and to "perverted fertility" resulting in overpopulation, as well as to a fermenting agent, (soda, but of the social kind), with additional possible reference to soil (sod), or even Sodom, as a synonym for promiscuity. The idea of overpopulation is further strengthened by the second line, hinting also at the possibility of soil depletion, or exhaustion. Vulcan, of course, is a god of fire; of a ritual or sacrificial fire, as well as a funeral pyre.

The third line is the most enigmatic one of all, especially because of the context of the quatrain. Generally, Artemis is viewed as a quaint goddess of hunt, but having studied her symbolical character, as it appears in virtually all the mythological systems of the world, I view her as the defense aspect of Gaia, the Mother Earth. In this respect she can indeed be viewed as a huntress—but as a huntress of men.

Man, after all, stands on the top of the food chain as the "supreme hunter" who can track down and kill even the most powerful predators. As long as man acts as a responsible hunter, exercising his right within the confines of natural renewal, he can prosper in safety. However, if he wreaks havoc on nature, if he behaves as senseless predator and exploiter, nature strikes back at him, and the supreme hunter becomes the hunted animal, with the hunt eventually turning into a dreadful slaughter. And it is this slaughter, which has nothing to do with "regular" wars, that is referred to here as "A repeated return to the honors of Artemis." These 'honors' include, usually in a combination, floods, droughts, wars, plagues, famines, and asteroid impacts, that affect people not only worldwide, but also on an exceptionally massive scale. Interestingly enough, even in the myths this retribution is directly tied to man's inability to maintain ecological balance in the world. More specifically, it is tied to the destruction of forests, where Artemis nominally made her home, and to the mountain slopes, the traditional sources of water springs.

By being familiar with her background, I can state with confidence that, judging from the context, a number of other quatrains refer to Artemis, at least indirectly: "She who was cast out will return to reign ... More than ever will her time be triumphant." (6/74) Or: "The shining deed of the new old one exalted will be so great in the south and north ..." (10/69) "They will come to deliver the Prince of Dannemark, redeem his shame in the temple of Artemis ..." (4/27)

Although the Church canonized a certain St. Artemisa, it cast the real one out, with the rest of the natural religion. Yet, the European "witches" have, for a long time, continued her worship, continued believing in her power. The most striking "indirect" reference to Artemis can be found in quatrain 1/62:

> "What a great loss learning will suffer,
> before the cycle of Latona is completed:
> Fire, great floods, because of overly ignorant rulers.
> How many centuries until it is seen restored."

To explain: Latona, also known as Leda, or "Lady," was the symbolical mother of Artemis and Apollo. Of the two, Artemis was born the first, and as befitting a goddess, she was born fully grown, and assisted with the birth of her brother, the Sun god Apollo. But at this very moment we have run into a snag. Latona was a Moon goddess, and thus could have hardly given birth to a Sun god. Certainly not until the end of the Moon Age cycle, that is now, at last, upon us. The ancient people understood this predicament, which is why they created the myth the way they did—to make the later generations wonder. In this regard they have largely failed, because, since Plato's days, myths were treated as quaint, albeit a bit confused stories. They are not. Whatever confusion is found in them got there thanks only to human ignorance, which often "adjusted" these to suit their understanding.

To start with, Artemis was given a "twin" brother on purpose—to date the events portrayed in the myth, which places its emergence, and her 'birth', into the Age of Gemini, or Twins, which started about 8,500 years ago. This also means that their "mother," i.e. the Moon Age, was born a 'generation' earlier, during the previous astrological cycle, or the Age of Cancer, which started some 11,400 years ago. Interestingly enough though, in the astrological sense, the Moon rules the sign of Cancer, or Crab, a sign whose subjects are known to move forward in a seemingly "backward" or "sideways" motion.

Apollo, as a Sun god, and thus as a personification of the Sun Age, still causes more of a dilemma here—until we realize *he was not born YET!* And this will take a bit more explaining to do.

Latona, as Leda, is also known as the Goose that laid the Golden Egg, and the Golden Egg, in turn, is again the Golden Age, and thus Apollo. But this Golden Age, or the Age of the Sun, will not really shine its light upon mankind, until the later part of the 21st century. Of course, Apollo has been portrayed as a "living god," but his "deeds" were merely the weak solar aspects of human mind and spirit, stuck fast in the Moon Age. Also, while splendid temples were built in his honour, their very high priests were aware of the fact their god was not born yet, but was merely in the process of being born. This process in turn was often enough portrayed by the ancient artists on various objects. There the Golden Egg is presented as only emerging from the Goose. Or, as a child, from the womb of the Egyptian goddess Hathor, who used to be known as the self-created "Mother of every god and goddess," and upon whom Leda was modeled. To complicate the imagery even further, Hathor is also known as Sekhmet, the lion-headed huntress of men—which brings us right back to Artemis.

The completion of Latona's cycle, as referred to by Nostradamus, is then identical to the completion of the Moon cycle, the termination of Moon Age, at which time Latona will finally "give birth" to Apollo. In this respect Artemis was, and mainly will be in the near future, assisting with the birth of Apollo, although in a somewhat "ghoulish" way. But being of a dual nature, like all the ancient goddesses, she was also known as the goddess of childbirth, among her other attributes. The "child," in our context, is the future humanity.

The above are but some examples of symbols borrowed from ancient myths, and these come with no connection to astrology what-so-ever, except the odd name. With that out of the way, we can now concentrate on the key topics Nostradamus himself had concentrated on, when devising The Centuries, in the chapters "The Asteroid Impact," "The Flood," "The War of Survival," and on the relevant consequences.

THE ASTEROID IMPACT

The accuracy of Nostradamus' predictions is legendary. Some of them even include specific dates which have been verified. Others, though, are so nebulous that they could fit almost any time period and, of course, people have attempted to use them for all kinds of purposes, imputing dates to them, by adding or subtracting artificial figures.

About thirty years ago I did my "scientific experiment," by using his various quatrains to calculate, at least roughly, the demise of the Soviet empire, arriving at a date between 1990 and 1992, which turned out to be pretty close, only to realize much later that Nostradamus actually provided the precise figure in his Letter to Henry II.

There is one quatrain though, 10/72, which is also remarkably clear and precise, as far as the date is concerned. It reads:

> "A great king of terror will descend from the skies,
> the year 1999, seventh month,
> to resuscitate the great King of Angolmois.
> Around this time Mars will reign for the good cause."

Here, as you can see, we have a perfect example of how little help an exact date is, if we do not understand the rest of the riddling prophecy—and if the date itself turns out to be a dud as well. But all is not lost. As we shall see, the prophecy remains very much valid, only the date needs a 'bit' of an adjustment.

To Nostradamus' credit, we have to state that he was quite uncertain of it himself, and complained quite bitterly, in his famous "Letter" to Henry II, about the ever changing calendars. As if to "prove" the point, he puts forward conflicting dates for the "duration of the world," since "its creation," till the time of Jesus Christ. One time the figures add up to 4,757 years, the other to 4,092 years, which results in a discrepancy of some 665 years. That, I trust, is but an exaggeration, intended only to underline the problem at hand. However, such concerns, on the seer's part, while completely valid, also demonstrate that he drew upon some very ancient sources of unknown dating.

We know, for example, that Jews of the Jesus' period, in order to accommodate the predictions of their prophets, and to eliminate Herod the Great from history, had 'erased' 40 years from their calendar. Before that, the Egyptian and the Babylonian calendars were tempered with, and later the Roman one. In spite of all this, Nostradamus' estimate, for the initial stage of the most important turning point in human existence, is still within the corresponding region of time, reconfirmed by Bishop Ussher, Kepler and Newton.

It is known that the Babylonian astronomer Berossus, who lived during the third century B.C.E., offered a date corresponding to May 5, 2000, to be the end of our era. Obviously, we know that was not the case either. The next "available date" was provided for us by the ancient Mayans fell on December 21, 2012, which designated the once famous end of the Mayan "Long Cycle." But as it turned out, in spite its original promise and with 20/20 hindsight, one can even understand why. And the why of it is time, again.

The "Long Cycle" starting date is August 11, 3,114 B.C.E., or almost 1,400 years before the Mayas emerged as a cultural group and about 3,500 years before their classical period started, during which such sophisticated concepts could have been formulated.

There is also possibility the Mayas inherited their calendar from the Olmecs, who were on the scene 2,000 earlier. Even if true, the Olmecs, in turn, would have received the relevant information from somewhere else, and during the intervening eons the specific date was forgotten, just like it was everywhere else.

Yet, whatever the date might have been, even by objective scientific standards we do not have that much time left before natural causes would put a stop to our mad behavior. In the opinion of the late Jacques Cousteau, the famous oceanographer, the majority of all the sea-life is bound to be dead, and so will most of the tropical forests, according to James Lovelock of the Gaia fame. If that were to happen, we would soon start running out of oxygen to breathe, and then be cooked alive, with these two massive ecosystems out of "operation," and unable to absorb any more carbon dioxide, or to produce oxygen.

On the other hand, we need to consider the time period of the 5,200 years, that make up the Mayan "Great Cycle," rather important, as it is also claimed that when the "original" Great Cycle was devised, a war caused a country to cease to exist. And indeed, when we multiply the years of the Great Cycle by five, we obtain the figure of 26,000 years (ago), which would have marked the end of the previous Zodiac cycle—including the previous Age of Kali. It is most likely that period of time, that particular Age of Kali, to which the dreadful wars, described in the Indian epic "Mahabharata," refer to, and which portrayed the use of flying machines, of nuclear or other energy weapons. The myths from all over the world, that refer to this "conflict" as the "war of the gods," also state the entire planet was burning, that all life on it ceased to exist. (I discuss this situation in a much greater detail in the book *Space Gods & Angels*.)

In this cycle such horrors will be avoided, yet the current 'mighty' civilization will be terminated by other, almost equally powerful means, that are at Nature's disposal, which brings us back to Nostradamus' famous quatrain 10/72.

A good number of absurd, as well as fantastic and nonsensical interpretations were offered for the first and the third line of the said quatrain, mainly "borrowed" from the realm of science fiction. I "borrowed" mine from the realm of ecology and myth which, as you will see more and more, have a lot in common—and the results are 'startling', indeed.

From the quatrain itself, it is quite obvious that something terrible is going to take place, and that "something" will descend from the skies. Not plunge, nor hurtle or crash, but descend, suggesting a relatively gradual approach of this catastrophe—but one we shall not be able to avert. As you will see, this "something" will be a large meteorite. (To avoid confusion of referring to the same object as a meteorite, comet, meteor, or asteroid, depending on the body's composition and its distance from Earth, I will be using as a "generic" term the word asteroid throughout the text, regardless of the stages the body will be in.)

But how can an asteroid, that will cause a massive destruction, "resuscitate the Great King of Angolmois"? And who is this king?

To answer that question, I had to write this book. Not that the answer would be essentially too complex, but it will contain features from diverse fields of knowledge. Yet, having read the book, you will see that the answer, glorious and gruesome at the same time, will fit into a few fairly short and fairly simple sentences, that would hardly mean anything without absorbing all that will lead up to them.

But first, let us use Nostradamus' own text to establish the fact as he described it; that is the event of the descending asteroid, put into a proper context, where we shall be able to compare all the related quatrains. As we shall see, sometimes a group of quatrains in fact tell an entire, fairly complex story, as they do in this instance.

> "Appearing towards the Seven Stars,
> not far from Cancer, the bearded star …
> … mourn the great Rome, night dissipated." 6/6

The Seven Stars is the Great Dipper (Ursa Major), and the constellation of Cancer is located virtually next to it in the night sky. There the asteroid, the "bearded star," will be seen for the first time. Eventually, it will blaze so brightly, the "night (will be) dissipated." After the impact, the city of Rome will be destroyed.

> "When the solar eclipse occurs,
> the monster will be seen in broad daylight:
> All interpretations will differ,
> no expense will be spared, where none was allocated." 3/34

The "monster," as will clearly be seen later, refers in different words to the "Great King of Terror," that is the same asteroid. By recognizing the established context, the above quatrain becomes virtually self-explanatory, with the possible exception of the solar eclipse, which most likely is to take place during the year of the impact, and was calculated by Nostradamus for the year 1999. It took place over France on August 11, 1999, which would have corresponded to July 29, 1999 of the Julian calendar, used during Nostradamus' time. But it was not only a wrong year, but also a wrong season. To trigger an ice age, whose onset and progression the seer described at great length and detail, the asteroid will have to impact in winter, for the additional "knock on" effect. In fact, without realizing it, he mentions December in quatrain 9/37, as we shall see later.

The indicated asteroid, in an overtaking position, "will be seen in broad daylight," and obviously, the initial calculations will differ as to whether it will impact on land or in the sea, or whether it will just pass through the Earth's atmosphere, or even just "bounce off it." When the inevitable will become obvious, "no expense will be spared" to alleviate the worst consequences of the impact.

> "After great misery, humanity approaches a greater one,
> as the great cycle of Centuries is renewed:
> Plague, blood, milk, famine, iron & pestilence.
> In the sky is seen fire, dragging a trail of sparks." 2/46

Because of the reference to the "great cycle," this quatrain belongs into the given context as well. That also means that the "fire" seen in the sky, "dragging a trail of sparks," is referring to the same asteroid, from which small fragments "flake off," as it hurls through the atmosphere.

> "The great star burns for seven days.
> Above the clouds two suns appear ..." 2/41

This part of the quatrain in turn makes it fairly obvious that the asteroid will take a full week to "catch up" with the planet from its overtaking position, and to enter the planet's upper atmosphere, where it will shine like a second sun. From Greek mythology we know of another such celestial body, under the name of Phaeton, which impacted the planet about 4,000 years ago.

> "Very near Auch, Lectoure & Mirande
> a great fire tumbles from the sky for three nights.
> The cause appears very stupendous and marvelous.
> Shortly afterwards the earth will quake." 1/46

In this quatrain the great seer is telling us the asteroid, the "Great King of Terror will descend from the skies" for three days—after "catching up" with it for the previous seven days. It would seem that the people on Earth will observe this spectacle for a total of ten days, before the asteroid impacts the planet. When it does, the planet "will quake." No, not just a local earthquake, but a planet-quake, that most likely will last for days, as did the one 4,000 years ago, recorded by the ancient Egyptians. A complementary line in quatrain 2/52 states: "For several nights the Earth will shake."

With the help of few geographical hints contained in the above quatrain, as well as from other quatrains and sources, we can even chart, at least approximately, the final path of the asteroid to its impact site.

In quatrain 2/96 we read in the first two lines: "A burning torch in the sky at night near the end and source of the Rhone ..." Since he purposefully states "near the end," i.e. the estuary, "and the source of the Rhone," and based on other indicators, we can quite correctly assume the asteroid, as observed from southeastern France, the seer's vantage point, will be traveling in a roughly north-easterly direction.

Anton Johansson, the Norwegian fisherman / clairvoyant, with numerous verified predictions to his credit, said in 1914: "I saw two natural catastrophes. One was an unheard of hurricane, raging over two continents, and the other an immense earthquake, connected with the eruption of a volcano in the North Sea." However, these two catastrophes are in fact both a part of the same event. The "unheard of hurricane" will be caused by descend of the asteroid through the atmosphere, the "immense earthquake" is the aforementioned planet-quake, and the "volcano" is the impact site of the asteroid. As a part of this 'scenario', he also saw skyscrapers toppling, and the forests in eastern Canada set ablaze by the fire from the sky, heading for the impact zone north-east of Norway.

Nostradamus even provides us with the actual size of the asteroid, and the immediate aftereffect of its impact.

> "The great mountain, seven stadia round.
> After peace, war, famine, inundation.
> It will spread far, drowning great countries,
> even ancient & great foundations." 1/69

Seven stadia is a bit less than a mile, or about 1.5 kilometer. What is more important though is how we interpret the expression "round." In the strictest contemporary sense, it means a circumference, and as such is rendered by virtually all the translators, which would present us with an object of about 500 meters (yards) in diameter, capable of a fairly massive damage on a planetary scale, but not on the scale described by Nostradamus. From the grammatical structure of the sentence though, we can assume he in fact meant the informal "around," or "about," in the visual sense, which in turn would imply a diameter. Furthermore, an asteroid about 1.5 kilometer in diameter would seem 'ideal' for the foretold consequences, considering also the time of the year and the place of the impact.

These consequences, briefly outlined in the first three lines of the quatrain 1/69 above, and elaborated on in greater details in many other quatrains, are indeed going to be shattering and take place on a worldwide scale, as amply hinted at in quatrain 2/62:

> "Mabus will soon die, then
> a dreadful destruction of people and animals:
> Suddenly a vengeance will come to rule.
> Thirst and hunger, hundred time stronger when the comet comes."

The name Mabus is one of several anagrams for Saturn, (here Sabum), which Nostradamus resorts to quite often in The Centuries. The "vengeance," for a lack of a better expression, is the "vengeance" of Nature for the mistreatment received. Still, as we will see later on, this is not a vengeance in the retaliatory human sense, but a part of the ongoing evolutionary process.

Quatrain 5/59 consists again of two unrelated halves. The second one reads: "Many will die because of Mars (War), introduced the day when a bearded star falls in Artois." The "bearded star," of course, is the same asteroid, mentioned in quatrain 2/46 as "fire, dragging a trail of sparks." The expression "Artois" is referring to the Arctic. The contemporary expression for the Northern Polar Region was originally derived from the Latin name for the constellation of the Great Bear, positioned almost directly above the North Pole, and bear in Latin is Arctos, from which have developed the names for both Artemis and King Arthur.

In other words, Nostradamus confirms that the asteroid in question will indeed impact in the Arctic. And, as we will see, the choice of that site is not at all accidental.

The impact is going to be a mighty one, and most likely will take place during the time night enshrouds Europe. In quatrain 2/91 we are told about it:

> "At sunrise a great fire will be seen,
> noise and light hover over the North:
> Around the globe death & cries are heard.
> Through weapons, fire and famine, death attends to them."

In the first two lines, once more, we have a confirmation about the site of the impact zone: "the North," or the North Pole region. This is further ascertained in quatrain 5/96: "The rose upon the middle of the world." The "rose," in this context, is the column of smoke and dust rising over the North Pole—"the middle of the world," in reference to the polar axis.

The Mayan prophecies predicted a very "similar" event: "A new day shall dawn in the north … The First Tree is restored: it is displayed to the world." Indeed, one can concede that, from a distance, this "nuclear" type explosion will resemble both, the rose, as well as a strange tree.

The consequence of this extraordinary event is also alluded to in quatrain 2/92: "Fire of the golden color seen from the sky on earth, struck by the high born one, a marvelous event …" In quatrain 1/87 it is again the first and the last line that correspond to the context: "Earthshaking fire from the centre of the Earth … "

The quatrain 1/87 is describing the enormous upwelling of magma and fire shooting from the impact crater in the Arctic, referred to as Aretusa, the ancient goddess of volcanoes. Yet this act, as clearly indicated, is caused by the Supreme Being, the "high born one" of quatrain 2/92. The "centre of the earth" is a yet another reconfirmation of the impact site: a polar region. Because the polar axis runs through polar regions, and the Earth revolves around this axis, they are viewed as the "centre" of the world.

The first two lines in quatrain 1/84 read: "The moon obscured in deep gloom, her brother turns a bright red in color …" We can also read a virtually identical prediction in the Bible: "… after the great tribulation of those days the sun will be darkened, and the moon will not give its light …" (Mat.13-40)

Such observations have been made, locally, after powerful volcanic eruptions, when the nearby atmosphere was saturated with dust and gases. The above described situation though will be observed at least over the entire northern hemisphere, and most likely all over the planet, due to the enormous quantities of dust and gas the asteroid's impact will deliver to the planet's atmosphere.

In quatrain 5/35, which refers essentially to later events, the first two lines read: "For the free city of the great crescent sea, which still carries the stone in its stomach …" After some puzzling I realized that "the great crescent sea" in fact is the Arctic Ocean, formed by the great arc of Siberia and Alaska. The "stone," of course, is the symbolic remnant of the asteroid, located somewhere in the Arctic Ocean.

> "A very great famine (caused) by a pestilent wave.
> It will extend its long rain the length of the Arctic …" 6/5

To comprehend what this part of the above quatrain is saying, we have to take a short detour through some ancient Egyptian, Israeli, and other records, referring to the impact of the asteroid in north-western Africa, some 4,000 years ago. Caius Julius Solinus left this message for posterity: "Following the deluge which is reported to have occurred in the days of Ogyges," (i.e. 24th century B.C.E.), "a heavy night spread over the globe for nine consecutive days." (Another translation gives the period as nine months which, as we will see, is probably closer to the truth.) Saint Augustine writes in his City of God (8/8): "Minerva (Athene) is reported to have appeared ... in the time of Ogyges," which, of course, represents a slight misdating. The Babylonians refer to the same asteroid as Ishtar. "The blazing fire which rains upon the hostile land, I am Ishtar." The ancient Greeks remember it in the myth of Phaeton, a "son" of the Sun god, who rode his father's fiery chariot and "fell to Earth." Yet, the Phaeton's name means "the blazing star," i.e. an asteroid. The ancient Chinese text, known as The Soochow Astronomical Chart, says of the same event: "(It) was visible in full daylight and, while moving across the sky, rivaled the sun in brightness."

As aforementioned, the ancient records also portray the aftermath of the asteroid's impact. The Egyptian manuscript *Ipuwer* states at various places: "Trees are destroyed ... No fruits no herbs are found ... Grain has perished on every side ... that has perished which yesterday was seen ... The towns are destroyed ... Upper Egypt has become dry ... Gates, columns, and walls are consumed by fire. The sky is in confusion ... The land is not light." (I.e. The land is dark.)

On the monolith of El Arish, dating from the Ptolemaic era, it says of the same event: "The land was in great affliction. Evil fell on this earth ... Nobody left the place for nine days, and during the nine days of upheaval there was such a tempest that ... men ... could (not) see the faces of their next."

L. Ginzberg, drawing on Joseph Flavius, Philo of Alexandria and rabbinical sources, stated the following: "An exceedingly strong west wind lasted for seven days. All this time the land was shrouded in darkness. On the fourth, fifth and sixth days, the darkness was so dense that they (the Egyptians) could not stir from their place. None was able to speak or hear, their outward senses in a trance."

The *Ipuwer Papyrus* also cries out: "Oh that the earth would cease from noise and (it) be no more," referring to the planet-quake.

The psychological effect on the people, especially in the Middle

East and in Egypt, who were in the flight path of the asteroid, and rather close to the impact site in today's Republic of Chad, must have been terrifying, considering they were quite ignorant of the cause, or the reason for this occurrence, and totally unprepared for it. One can only hope that we will fare better, once the events predicted for our era will be taking place, because they will be equally awesome and terrifying.

Now, a comment, in a somewhat retrograde fashion, is required on what transpired those roughly 4,000 years ago. This "noise" refers to the vibrations emitted by the Earth's solid lithosphere, after it was impacted by the asteroid, analogous to the "moonquake" that took place after the Moonlander alighted on that celestial body. The "exceedingly strong west winds," and the days of darkness, refer to the "sandblasting" effects of dirt particles, driven by continuous, extremely powerful hurricanes, unleashed by the combined forces of the hot body passing through the atmosphere, and the explosion upon impact. The discrepancy in the number of days is merely coloured by religious preferences. While most Mediterranean people, including the Egyptians, held the number three, or its multiples, to be of sacred significance, for the Jews it was the number seven.

The "... pestilent wave (which) will extend its rain the length of the Arctic," as predicted by Nostradamus for our near future in quatrain 6/5, will be caused by the same "sandblasting" effect of the ejecta from the impact zone, spreading outwards. It is also possible the asteroid will deliver microbes, causing a pestilence. For example plague.

Furthermore, impacts by fairly sizable asteroids are a lot more common than most astronomers were, until recently, willing to admit. Now, some of them claim such impacts happen, on average, every 3,000 years, which seems to correspond to the intervals between the latest four such impacts. In addition to the one already mentioned, a sizable impact took place about 5,200 years ago in the Antarctic, a third one along the North American seaboard, about 10,200 years ago, and another one, circa 13,500 years ago, in the Hudson Bay.

However, while the four previous impacts were intended only to cool the planet down to the level preceding the fairly sudden global "warm-ups," the goal of the impact predicted by Nostradamus is qualitatively very different. Where the previous impacts were "only" intended to maintain life, and the climatic "status quo" on this planet, the coming one is intended, as we shall see, not only to change the current "status quo," but to finalize the Guided Evolution of mankind, which would be impossible without an ice age, and the accompanying upheavals.

The impact predicted by Nostradamus, and other seers, is bound to vaporize, upon impact, hundreds of cubic kilometers of seawater, and 200 to 500 cubic kilometers of rock dust and other ejecta. The dust will shoot up some 40 kilometers into the space, way above the atmosphere, and remain there for months, some of the finer particles even for years. The spreading of the dust shield, along with the increased cloud cover from the vaporized water over the Earth, especially its northern half, will lead to an "asteroid winter," or an instant full blown ice age, as deep layers of snow will start accumulating even during the summer months.

Such an intervention by the Supreme Being must not just be seen as a "punishment" for our stupidity, but as a saving measure intended to protect the Life at large, including the human life, from perishing, most likely forever, if this civilization was allowed to continue with its insane "experiment."

In either case, from the examples provided here so far, we can conclude that life on this planet is perilous, at times. But it would not have to be as perilous, as it occasionally gets, if people heeded the warnings they are given, which they do not. Such a disregard is not only recorded in the biblical story of the Flood, but also in the much older Sumerian writings, and in the relevant myths from all over the world.

Before we part company with this chapter though, I would like to return to the line "to resuscitate the Great King of Angolmois," found in quatrain 10/72, and attempt to explain it.

By now we have sufficiently established that the "great king of terror" is the asteroid that will come to resuscitate the Great King. The outstanding problem is the name "Angolmois." In my opinion, this 'name' most likely combines within itself the words "angel," and the old French word "moite," or "a half," but which also designates two unilateral units of a tribe. We can also distinctly identify in that expression the French word "moi," as in "me" or "mine." When we combine all these possible meanings, we arrive at an expression suggesting something like "my angelic half," which is likely alluding to a mental upgrade of the deservedly surviving portion of the future humanity, once the full effect of the ice age will become established, to the level lost during the tragic massive warming, that started circa 11,700 years ago. Even Jesus implied, in a round-about way, that people will be like angels, like gods. (Mat. 22 - 30, 5 - 48)

The "Mars (reigning) for a good cause" merely suggests the coming hecatombs will not be cruelly pointless, but will serve a specific and good cause. As Nostradamus states in his Letter to Henry II: "I readily confess that all emanates from God and ... that I have mixed in no divination coming from fate, but from God, from nature ..." And yet, it has to be said over and over again, our destiny, our fate, its ultimate outcome, has been decided by the Supreme Being, who, at the same time, is also inseparable from nature, as mentioned by Nostradamus.

As to the actual date of the impact, I would hazard to say that, due to the critically worsening climatic situation, it cannot be too far off. And since it needs to take place in winter, when the solar eclipse is also visible, the choices are rather limited.

They include March 20, 2015, which is technically the last day of winter, that is getting progressively warmer, but this eclipse will be visible in Europe – if that is at all important. The next possible dates are March 9, 2016, February 26, 2017, along with February 15, 2018 and January 6, 2019. Somewhat more promising dates include December 26, 2019, December 14, 2020 and December 4, 2021. Other than that, there are two to three solstices taking place on the planet, year after year.

While contemplating THE date, we also have to consider the ancient tradition of Saturnalia, known mainly from Rome and Persia, held around the time of winter equinox practically all around the world, including the Americas, which foreshadowed the future social, ecological, as well as mental changes. To comply with this tradition, the last three dates would indeed seem the most suitable ones, as the Saturnalia usually started on December 13.

THE FLOOD

The impact of the asteroid, as already stated, is going to displace enormous amounts of seawater. Much of it will instantly evaporate, but most of it will transform the imparted kinetic energy into an incredible mega tsunami, destined to circumnavigate the globe. Upon reaching a shore, any shore, this "wave" could easily rear up to be 1,000 meters high, or higher, and roar very deep inland. In flat coastal areas it will travel for up to hundreds of kilometers beyond the seashores.

It will first sweep around the Arctic Ocean, but will not be contained by it. Turning south through the Atlantic Ocean, as well as through the Bering Strait, and Pacific Ocean, the deadly wave will be headed for the Antarctic, to dislodge the ice shelves, surrounding that continent and / or resting upon it, but already weakened by the hot house effect, as well as the planet-quake, caused by the impact.

However, these ice shelves will not be dislodged at the same time, but in seven stages. (See 3/10 below.) As this tsunami will hit the shore there, it will most likely first dislodge the Ross Ice Shelf, the one most vulnerable to such an assault, but also the most critical one, because it supports in position several other ice fields on the continent behind it. Once such an ice field plunges into the ocean, it will in turn create a mega tsunami wave as well, and most of these will match, or exceed, the effect of the first wave, with one critical difference: Since the plunging of each one of them would rise the global sea level by several meters, or even tens of meters, the successive tsunamis would always hit the shores at higher and higher elevations, reaching still further and further inland. Similar effect will also be wrought upon the ice fields in Greenland.

> "With blood & famine even greater calamity.
> Seven times it approaches the shore … "   3/10

That the above part of the quatrain also refers to the mega tsunamis, and the Flood, discussed here, is further confirmed by the following quatrain, and many other.

> "For a long time the place will cherish peace & plenty.
> Then, throughout the kingdom, France is deserted:
> Bodies, dead by water, brought to the shores,
> waiting in vain for the chance to be buried."   4/20

Several other quatrains will help to explain the reason for the situation described above, starting with the first two lines of quatrain 2/22.

> "The escaping army will depart from Europe,
> joining up near the submerged island … "

The submerged island, upon closer examination, turns out to be Britain. More to the point though, much of this island is less than 100 meters above the current sea level, which would lead one to conclude that the sea level will rise, in seven quick steps, by about 100 meters. That would also mean that virtually all the polar ice fields and glaciers will be gone at that stage. This indeed is confirmed by the first two lines of quatrain 3/70:

> "Great Britain, especially England,
> will be inundated to a great depth …"

The reconfirmation of the extent of this Flood can be found in the first two lines of quatrain 5/87:

> "In the year Saturn sheds his servitude,
> the Frankish territory to be inundated with water …"

Here, by "the Frankish territory," is most likely implied not only France itself, but also Holland, Belgium, as well as Germany, that were all lorded over, one time or another, by the Germanic Franks. And having said all of this, we can now return to the image from quatrain 4/20: "… the kingdom of France deserted … bodies … waiting in vain … to be buried." The fact is, there will be no one left alive in those regions to bury the millions of dead bodies. After all, much of the terrain along the western shores of continental Europe is also located less than 100 meters above the sea level and the mountain-sized tsunamis are going to reach very deep inland. Thus only those who either live, or were able to reach the safety of the deep, mountainous interior of the continent(s), will be able to survive. But these people will suddenly find themselves hard pressed by their own existential problems, and will not be in the position to worry about burring dead bodies, hundreds of kilometers away from them. The time period for this situation is also clearly indicated: "In the year Saturn sheds his servitude," that is the year following the impact by the asteroid. This message in turn is reinforced by quatrain 8/29:

> "The fourth pillar, dedicated to Saturn,
> split by earthquake & flood.
> Under the Saturnian structure a broken urn.
> The gold Capion took & then restored."

The "fourth pillar" is the fourth age, that is our age, the Age of Iron, "dedicated," in a sacrificial sense, to Saturn. This "pillar" will be "split," and shattered, ended, by the aforementioned planet-quake, and the Flood we are discussing here. "The gold Capion took & then restored" will be found in the bowls of "the Saturnian structure." That is of the Saturnian Age. The gold in the "broken urn" represents the restoration of the "Golden Age." In this context it hardly matters who, or what, the name Capion represents. Most likely, it is a hybrid name, combining the concepts of a "head," (caput), or rather what is in it, and "champion," but pointing still to Saturn.

Nostradamus also makes it fairly plain that this Flood will be sudden and virtually continuous.

> "Very near the Tiber hurries death,
> a short while before a great flood.
> The captain of the ship taken, put into bilges,
> castle and palace in flames." 2/93

The name of the river, Tiber, makes it obvious the "castle and the palace" is the Vatican, and that the "captain" is the Pope, the "ship" being the "bark" of St. Peter. The quatrain predicts the Pope will be killed by an enraged mob that suddenly realized the God's promise of "no more floods," contained in the Bible, was a sham, and will clamor for a sacrificial lamb to die before they do. Still, the second line is ultimately the most important one in this quatrain, because it informs us that it will be a GREAT Flood, and that it will be sudden. This fact is then being repeated in quatrain 8/16:

> "At the place where Hieron had his ship built,
> there will be such a great sudden flood,
> that one will not have a place nor land to take a refuge in.
> The waters mount the Olympic Fesulan."

The core message is spelled out for us in the two middle lines. The rest is a "mere decoration," albeit with supplementary information. The Hieron almost certainly is the original model for all "heroes," that is for every person dedicated to the service of the Earth goddess Hera, and his name was Hercules. He was also the original Saviour, hoary with age, linked to the revival of cultures, that were, like him, or the Phoenix, perennially reborn out of their own ashes, or ruins. Ultimately, he is also associated with the "renewal of the Ages," and "in charge" of delivering the new Golden Age.

Also, since Dubrovnik (Ragusa), in today's Croatia, is "the city holy to Hieron," as Nostradamus tells us in quatrain 10/63, we can assume it is the same place where he "had his ships built," because the same place, under different names, has been a port for millennia. The coastal area there, backed by steeply rising mountains, is obviously destined to be completely covered by the sea.

In my opinion, the phrase "Olympic Fesulan" refers to the site of the ancient Olympic Festivals in Greece, that we call, in a somewhat limiting sense, "Olympic Games." According to my (The Times) Atlas of the World, this site is more than 100 meters above the sea level, which is how high "the waters will mount" at that place, without necessarily staying there.

The idea of the planet-quake, hinted at in quatrain 8/29, is further elaborated on in quatrain 9/31:

> "The trembling of the earth in Montara,
> the tin island of St. George half sunk ..."

Montara most likely refers to Scandinavia, that consist mainly of mountains, and near which the asteroid can be expected to impact. The "island of St. George" is England, named after this saint protector. It too is located fairly close to the impact zone, and sits atop a fault line connected to it. At the same time, this quatrain only reinforces what we were told in quatrain 3/70: "Great Britain, especially England, will be inundated to a great depth." Thus, if one can be allowed to speculate, as a result of the combined effects of the planet-quake, and of the Flood, England will end up being covered by about 100 meters of water. The same, depending on the geological situation, would happen in other places as well.

However, there are quatrains that provide us with much greater details, concerning the impending fate of the British islands and its people.

> "Great efforts will be made in the north.
> Above the ocean a gate will be opened.
> The rule will be re-established on the island.
> The appearance of the veil will make London tremble." 2/68

> "Towards Aquitaine, from the British islands.
> By them also a great incursion ..." 2/1

The references in these two linked quatrains are quite unmistakable. The "great efforts" will be made in Britain, to save as many people as possible. As the second line suggests, "a gate will be opened," not so much "above the ocean," as above the islands, situated in the ocean. This "gate" will turn out to be an air-bridge to a high ground in France—the Pyrenees mountains and the Aquitaine region there. The last line tells us about the people who will be left behind in London, and elsewhere. Understandably, they will tremble, seeing the plume, or the "veil" of the asteroid, streaming almost directly overhead. They will know they are as good as dead. The third line is getting ahead of the time-line, telling us that, fairly soon afterwards, some of the refugees will return to what will be left of Britain, namely parts of Scotland and Wales.

> "In quarrel the rule divided between brothers,
> to take up the arms & the name of Britain.
> The titular English advised to be on guard.
> Surprise out of the night, conducted by air to France." 8/58

The last line confirms the idea of the air-bridge, established after "the surprise" of the asteroid impact is announced, mere days before it takes place. The "brothers" are the two groups of the British, of which the "titular English" in Aquitaine are "advised to be on guard," probably in the light of Nostradamus' predictions, that foretell of their heroism, but also of their gradual reduction throughout The War, and their eventual total demise.

The penetrating effect of the mega tsunami is sketched out for us in quatrain 9/37:

"Bridge & mills toppled in December,
so very high will mount the Garonne:
Walls, buildings toppled in Toulouse,
so that none will know his place before Matronne."

It will not be the river Garonne that will "mount" so high, as to smash bridges, factories, (i.e. the "mills"), walls, and all kinds of other buildings, including apartment blocks and offices, but the raging tsunami, roaring in about 300 kilometers from the sea, to demolish the city so badly that none will be able to recognize the place, after the "Matronne" will be done with it. The image of the "Matronne" corresponds here to the punitive aspect of "the Lady," or "Mother Earth," that we know as Artemis, or Kali, among other names.

We also need to take note here of the critical discrepancy in Nostradamus' timing of the impact, the direct cause of this tsunami. In quatrain 10/72 he is predicting it will happen in July 1999, which it did not. Here though, probably unaware of the relationship, he is talking about December, the month selected by the Mayans for the end of the cycle. Or rather the beginning of the end.

"Because of the overflow of the Ebro, Po, Tagus, Tiber & Rhone,
and because of the pond Le Mans & Arezzo,
the two grand & chief cities of Garonne
taken, dead, drowned. Human booty divided." 3/12

The named cities are to be found in France and Italy, deep in the interior. The "two grand & chief cities of Garonne" are Bordeaux and Toulouse. The "overflow" of all the named rivers, and of the "pond," that is of the sea, all have their origin in the tsunami wave, and in the rise of the sea level.

To complete the picture of devastation for the French, Nostradamus also alluded to the fate of their capital city in quatrain 9/82:

"By the flood & mighty plague
the great city is assailed for a long time ..."

The "great city," of course, is Paris. Being situated 'mere' 200 kilometers from the sea shore, as the crow flies, and only 20 odd meters above the sea level, Paris would most likely end up being even more devastated than Toulouse, and thus it would be hard to imagine anyone could survive there, and suffer from a plague. However, it is possible people will venture there, or be sent there later, to salvage, or to loot, the accumulated historical treasures, and other valuables. But if they will get tempted to drink the water there, they will most like become afflicted by a "plague" of typhoid and die, because all the water treatment plants in all the inundated cities will be contaminated from the flooded sewers, and by the decomposing bodies of people and animals, as well as by various chemicals. Nostradamus also states quite clearly in quatrain 3/84:

> "The great city will be soon quite deserted,
> not a single one of its inhabitants will remain ..."

He is equally to the point in quatrain 6/43:

> "For a long time it will remain uninhabited
> where Seine & Marne will gush forth ..."

And Paris is located between these two rivers. Nostradamus also brings our attention to the chaotic climate, afflicting much of the world during the transition period from the hothouse era to the next ice age, using Italy as an example, in quatrain 3/52:

> "In Campania a long period of rain,
> and in Apulia a great drought ..."

We are even told that the time frame for this climatic shift will be forty years, in quatrain 1/17:

> "For forty years the rainbow will not be seen,
> for forty years it will be seen every day:
> The dry earth will further desiccate,
> and there will be great floods when it is seen."

Such extreme conditions, as already suggested, will not be taking place in the same location, successively, but concurrently, in different regions, as suggested by quatrain 3/52 above. Other references to the unsettled climate can be also found in quatrains 2/3, 2/84, 4/69, 5/76, 5/98, 6/79, and 10/6.

To reconfirm the presence of a common original source, we should point out that the New Testament (Mat. 24-37) also maintains that "the coming of the Son of Man will be just like the days of Noah." Incongruously enough, this rather avoided statement in fact also predicts an "annulment" of the non-existent Covenant, Noah is said to have received from Yahweh.

Within days of the impact, the Flood will change the topography of the continents almost beyond recognition. In Europe, much of England will be gone, as will large portions of France, Germany,

Finland, and Poland. Holland and Denmark will all but disappear from the map. But so will Florida, and large portions of the states on the Gulf coast, and along the eastern seaboard of the United States, as well as large chunks of real estate on the West Coast. In Canada, Prince Edward Island will disappear, as will all of the low lying regions in the Atlantic provinces. Victoria and Vancouver, on the West Coast, will be but a painful memory. Even the inland cities of Montreal, Ottawa and Toronto will most likely be critically affected by the tsunamis, and the Flood.

Looking at the map of the world will tell you the rest of the story: All the inhabitable parts of Japan will be under water, or devastated. The historical heartland of China will be under water, along with most of its food producing regions. All of the South-East Asia, including Australia and New Zealand will be devastated, the most populous and productive regions under water. Bangladesh will be gone, as will be the large food producing, and densely populated regions of India, Pakistan and Egypt. A new large inland sea will form in southern Russia and the Ukraine. In South America, most of the immense, oxygen producing Amazon forest will be a large inland sea as well. Uruguay will be obliterated, and the populous, productive eastern part of Argentina will be gone as well, along with all the other extensive low lying regions on that continent.

The global population losses, from the Flood alone, will be in tens, and most likely in the hundreds of millions. Then the monster storms will arrive, and the 'freaky' weather, hinted at in numerous quatrains, not to speak of the months and months of eerie darkness and cold, immediately following the impact. Then the "asteroid winter" will start setting in. But, as the precipitation, in form of snow, starts accumulating near the north and south poles, increased desiccation will effect more and more the subtropical and tropical regions of the planet, already enough devastated by the heat caused draught, threatening with starvation most of the people who will live in the places most severely afflicted by this climatic swing.

Historically, people have responded only one way to such challenging conditions: by mass migrations, and by wars of survival. But these could just as well be called the wars of extinction. In quatrain 1/94 we read:

> "A new war arises from vengeance & remorse.
> The lady is honoured by the force of terror."

That "lady," again, can be called Artemis, Kali, Hathor, Sedna, or any other death dealing aspect of Gaia. Yet, as 'crazy' as it might seem, there is nothing Darwinistically haphazard about such situations, because they are all a part of our Guided Evolution, which topic is discussed in the chapter "Spirit Reborn."

This summary, of sorts, again demonstrates that this event will merely open the major transformative door for mankind, and that it is not some kind of 'magical' and painless moment, as envisioned and hoped for by many adherents of the so called "New Age thinking."

THE WAR OF SURVIVAL

In this chapter I will be drawing information from some 200 quatrains that demonstrably refer to that specific series of events. Yet, there are at least 100 other quatrains that refer to the same topic, in a more "peripheral" manner, and another 100 or so, that most likely broach upon the subject as well. In other words, about 40 percent of Nostradamus' predictions, perhaps even more, are dedicated to this coming War. A figure out of all proportions, considering his book, The Centuries, contains less than 1,000 quatrains. But then, this War will be out of all proportions, when compared to any other war we know of.

Furthermore, if we were to add to this number all the other quatrains we use in this book, we would have to realize that the vast majority of Nostradamus' predictions deal with the next several decades of the 21st century, that in fact the entire book was written for the sake of this generation, and for no other purpose. But in order to reach us, "no ambiguities ... have been inserted, but all rather kept under a cloudy obscurity," confined the master in his Letter to Henry II, where he also states: "I neither could nor would explain them clearly. Never the less, in order to make comprehensible certain facts that are horrible strokes of destiny, some of them had to be delineated." He also states in the same Letter that these events "are to transpire soon." Of course, the very word "soon" was somewhat obscuring the fact that centuries were meant, which he himself stated in quatrain 1/62.

In either case, Nostradamus was making it as plain as possible that his predictions were essentially meant for our specific period of time, and that, barring certain exceptions, the quatrains depict our specific period of time, because this period represents the key intersection for the future destiny of mankind.

> "The gods will make it appear to mankind
> that they are authors of the great conflict ..." 1/91

What the two lines in fact say is that, obedient of their historical conditioning, the people of our era will think they are the originators of all the coming conflicts. But after the impact of the asteroid, this notion will gradually start changing. Unable to enter any theological debate, Nostradamus has risked quite a bit by evoking "the gods," when he meant the Supreme Being rather than Yahweh.

> "The cycle of the great number seven
> to appear at the times of the Games of Slaughter,
> not far from the start of the great millennial age,
> when the dead come out of their tombs." 10/74

> "The great theatre will be raised again;
> the dice thrown & the nets already cast.
> The chief tolling the death knell too tired
> to bow down to times long splitting." 3/40

These two quatrains make it even more obvious that Nostradamus had a much, much more momentous series of events in mind when he wrote them. They represent the key not only to the vast majority of quatrains dealing with battles and wars, but to his book of prophecies in general.

The line "The cycle of the great number seven" refers to the millennial count implicit in the Bible which, according to the esteemed calculations, reckons the "year of creation" to have been 4004 B.C.E. If so, then the seventh millennium, "the great number seven," started in 2005 C.E. And not far from that date will start "the Games of Slaughter" that we call here "the war of survival," that separates mankind from the real rewards of "the grand millennium." The last line of quatrain 10/74 is jumping ahead of the time-line somewhat, announcing, in a symbolical language, that the "dead," i.e. the living mankind, will rise from their millennia-long entombments of their mental / spiritual sleep.

The "great theatre" of quatrain 3/40 is but a synonym for the "Games of Slaughter." As the word "again" suggests, it will not be the first time such "performance" will take place during mankind's existence. However, according to the myths, it will be the last one, marking mankind's maturation. The quatrain further restates the fated inevitability of what is to take place, by saying that the "chief," i.e. Jupiter, the ruler of the passing age, will grow tired from reaping the abundant crop of death, while unable to prevent this situation from taking place, and unable to stop it. Myriads of human beings will have to reach the tear in the fabric of time, and tumble out of it, along with Jupiter.

The same lesson can be gleaned from the overall content of the Letter to Henry II. It was somewhat difficult to follow, until I realized the Letter in fact forms an "endless" loop, somewhat like the Mobius strip, of shuffled snippets of future history. While it also briefly mentions the French and the Russian revolutions, and adds a few other diversionary excursions, it concentrates predominantly on our immediate future. In fact, after excluding the obvious peripherals, one could reconstruct the skeletal outlines of the near future from this Letter alone. It even states that the physical source of the coming War, "the great empire of Antichrist will begin in Atilla and Xerxes and will descend in great and countless numbers …"

Here "Atilla" represents the regions of southwestern Siberia and of southern Russia and Ukraine, where the Huns have invaded Europe from. Xerxes, of course, represents Persia, or today's Iran. The quatrains only confirm this in a much greater detail.

> "The bird of prey flying for six months,
> before the French make preparations for the conflict.
> Some will regard it as a good omen, others as ambiguous, sinister.
> The weaker party will deem it a good prediction." 1/34

This "bird" most likely is a space satellite, able to see the ground again, after most of the dust ejected by the asteroid impact has settled down, some two years later. It will most likely be reporting movements of Russian and allied troops, the "Huns," heading for central and south-western Europe "for six months, before the French make preparations for the conflict." Obviously, the French, and the other West-European countries still capable of military action, will be tardy in their response, being too busy keeping what is left of their countries functioning, and keeping the surviving people alive, most likely by conflicting democratic means.

The last line of quatrain 5/35 reads: "To seize a branch, war opened by the great one." The seized "branch" is probably an array of Western military satellites, or satellites with a potential military function, knocked out by the Russians, "the great one," who are more often mentioned by Nostradamus, in connection with The War, than anybody else, with the exception of the Moslems. He introduces these two prime aggressors in this conflict in the two following quatrains:

"The rule of the two to last a very short time:
Three years & seven months pass, they go to war.
The two vestals rebel against them.
The victor then born on American soil." 4/95

"During the appearance of the comet,
three great princes will be made enemies.
Struck from the peaceful sky, earth trembles.
At Po, at Tiber, the serpent of inundation placed on the shore." 2/43

In spite the fact one quatrain mentions two parties to the conflict, and the other three, they are both describing the same War. In quatrain 4/95 the two parties are the Russians, along with their allies, confronting an undefined assortment of West-European countries. I am saying undefined, because, following the asteroid impact and the Flood, some will cease to exist, including Denmark, Holland, Britain, and Ireland, along with most of the inhabitable parts of Scandinavia. In fact quatrains 2/69 and 2/39 tell us exactly which countries will form the Western alliance.

"The French king through the Celtic skill
calms the noisy discord of the great monarchy,
flourishes his scepter over three partners,
against the leader of the great Hierarchy." 2/69

"A year before the Italian conflict,
Germans, French, Spanish for the strong one:
The schoolhouse of the republic will fall,
where, except for a few, they suffocate to death." 2/39

Unfortunately, because these quatrains are so interlocking and overlapping, a bit of confusion might arise, as we shunt among them. My only suggestion is to re-read the blocks of texts. In either case, the last two quatrains tell us that, in time of extreme crisis, democracy, i.e. "the schoolhouse of the republic," will not work, and will be replaced by a dictatorship, aka "monarchy," headed by a Frenchman, elected by an equally dictatorial representatives from Germany, Spain, and Italy to lead the Western alliance.

"The rule of the two," of quatrain 4/95, refers to the Russian and the French led alliances, who will go to war with each other three years and seven months after the asteroid's impact. In turn the phrase "the three great princes," of quatrain 2/43, refers to the already mentioned Russian and French led alliances, while the third one is Persia, or today's Iran. The motives for aggression, on the part of Russia and Persia, will be predominantly of ecological nature, driven by the urge to survive. Russia, for example, will be afflicted by an instant ice age and immense flooding, rendering over 90 percent of its territory uninhabitable, while Persia will suffer from permanent rain.

> "Rain, famine and war will not cease in Persia;
> too much trust will greatly betray the monarch:
> To finish in France what started there.
> A secret sign for one to be sparing." 1/70

The first line of the above quatrain is quite self-explanatory. The second one most likely has a double meaning: trust in the enterprise undertaken, as well as the trust in the associates. The third line probably refers to the rule of the mullahs, which started in France with Ayatollah Khomenni. The last line essentially speaks of a 'premonition': If you mistreat, torture and kill, you in turn will be mistreated, tortured and killed, when the time comes.

> "From the Black Sea & the great Tartary
> a king will come to see France,
> penetrating through Turkey & Armenia,
> and leave his bloody rod in Istanbul." 5/54

> "For fire & weapons, not far from the Black Sea,
> the Persian will come to occupy Trabzon.
> Pharos and Lesbos tremble, the Sun in allegro;
> the waters of Adriatic covered with Arab blood." 5/27

> "The great Satyr & Tiger of Hyrcenia
> will present a gift to those of the Ocean.
> A commander of the fleet will sail from Carmania,
> to take the land of the Phoenicians, in Tyre." 3/90

This "quatrain overload" is necessary, in order to demonstrate how they are interlinked and how they overlap. For example, the quatrain 5/27 tells us the Persians will occupy the Turkish port of Trabzon, near the present Iranian border, which will place the Persians on the shores of the Black Sea. Armenia is also on the Iranian northern border, as are the regions of "the great Tartary," which is today's Turkmenistan. Once situated there, the Persian leader from Hyrcenia, on the Caspian Sea, located in the same northern region, "will present a gift to those of the Ocean," i.e. the navy. Yet, while Iran has a navy, it is not really an ocean-going navy, but serves mainly a coastal defense function. In that part of the world only the Russians, and to a certain extent the Ukrainians, have an ocean-going navy. Thus, most likely, he will present the gift to the Russian navy, perhaps of a port facility, since Russia will, once again, be the leader of an east-European coalition.

In return for the "gift," whose nature remains uncertain, but most likely will also include a non-aggression pact, Persia will not only receive a fleet of warships, but also a large store of weapons from the Russians, mentioned in quatrain 5/27. However, it is also quite likely that the Persians will capture caches of American weapons and planes located at the U.S. bases there, as well as a large part of the Turkish arsenal, possibly the very plant manufacturing the American designed F-16 fighter-jets. It is also possible the Persians will acquire the needed warships from India, which indeed is attempting to create an ocean-going navy, because these two countries are developing close ties, which also include military purchases and scientific co-operation.

Having conquered all of Turkey, as per quatrain 5/54, Persia will turn its attention to southern Europe, to the Middle East, and possibly also to North Africa, as suggested by quatrains 5/27 and 3/90. The names mentioned, such as the island of Lesbos, the port of Tyre, or Pharos, in Egypt, are merely of symbolical value, indicating only the general locality, or region, because all of these named places will be submerged by the sea. Incidentally, these Arab targets will be attacked by a Persian fleet sailing "from Carmania," on the Persian Gulf, around the Arabian Peninsula, and up the submerged Suez Canal. In fact it is quite possible the Persians could end up with two substantial fleets.

The "Sun in allegro" is just a poetic expression for indicating that the events will start moving very fast, or allegro, in musical terms, towards their eventual "solar" resolution.

> "The chief of Persia will replenish the great Colchis—
> the Trirame fleet against the Arab people.
> From Parthia & Media & to pillage the Cyclades.
> Then a long rest at a great Ionian port." 3/64

Colchis, the home of the fabled "Golden Fleece," is located in the south-eastern corner of the Black Sea, near the port of Trabzon. It will be (re)populated by the Persian people. Parthia and Media are both regions in Persia. From all those places the Persians will attack the Arab targets, as well as the Cyclades, an archipelago of Greek islands in the Aegean Sea, separating Turkey and Greece. The last line of the above quatrain implies the conquest of Greece, since the Ionian coast is in the north-western part of Greece, and this conquest is confirmed by the last line of quatrain 2/96, stating: "Persia will turn and invade Macedonia," situated just west of Greece. To pinpoint exactly which port the seer had in mind is all but impossible, since all the existent ports will be inundated. Most likely the Persians will construct a brand new port of their own there.

Furthermore, the "long rest" most likely will also be enforced, because, based on at least a couple of quatrains, we can suspect the Persians will have suffered a serious setback at that stage, which will force them to regroup and reorganize in the Balkans.

> "After a rest, voyaging for Epirus.
> A great relief sent to Antioch.
> The black-haired one to tighten strongly grip on Empire.
> Brazen Barbarian to roast on a spit." 1/74

> "A new rage upon the fleet near the Adriatic sea.
> The earth trembles, pushed into the air, it falls back.
> Egypt trembles, (but) Arab (power) grows.
> A Herald is sent to call for assistance in the east." 2/86

Epirus is a region in the north-western part of Greece, featuring also the Ionian coast and the future Persian port. Antioch is a city in southern Turkey. This reference is most likely tied to quatrain 3/64, which speaks volumes of raids and pillaging elsewhere, carried out in the attempt to supply their own people with provisions. The explanation for the barbarian roasted on a spit comes in the subsequent quatrain, numbered 2/86. It is virtually certain it describes the use of a nuclear weapon against a fleet, the "new rage"in the conflict. It will most likely be launched by the Western alliance, in order to prevent the Persians from heading for Italy.

Of course the loss of a fleet would represent a major setback for the Persians, and open the window of opportunity for the Arabs. For this reason the frontline Persian armies will send a high-ranking messenger back east for help. As the quatrains 4/95 and 2/43 suggest, the Russian and the Persian attack on Europe will take place almost simultaneously, and the two bodies of eastern armies will be heading westwards, virtually parallel to each other.

> "The horrible war will be prepared in Europe —
> the following year the pestilence will come,
> so very horrible that young, old, even animals (will die).
> Blood, fire, Mercury, Mars, Jupiter in France." 9/55

This "horrible war" could hardly be blamed directly on Europe, unless by Europe was meant mainly the Russian alliance. The only way Western Europe could be blamed for "preparing" the war, is for having more food supplies, for being able to organize itself better and faster, and eventually for receiving food shipments from North America. On the other hand, "the horrible war" could be a reference to the first use of a nuclear weapon in this conflict, conducted by the Europeans, possibly by the French who rely so heavily on the "nuclear deterrent." If so, then this event will take place about a year before the fairly substantial use of nuclear weapons in Western Europe by the Russians, which the third line of the above quatrain is most likely alluding to, calling the after-effect of the nuclear explosions "the pestilence." Mercury here stands for transformation, Mars for war, and Jupiter for the pains of the passing Age.

> "He who will hold the government of the great cloak
> will be led to execute in certain cases.
> The twelve red ones will spoil the cover,
> under murder, murder will be perpetrated." 4/11

The symbology of the great cloak of protection is very ancient. Here Nostradamus applies it to the government of "the twelve red ones," that is of Russia and its allies. However, the pretence of mutual protection will soon be betrayed by the often murderous behaviour, probably carried out under a cloak of murderous secrecy. At least initially.

"Weak galleys will be joined together.
The strongest of the false enemies at the rampart.
The weak assailed, Wroclaw trembles,
Lubeck and Meissen take the barbarian side." 9/94

"Weak galleys" are the weak ships of small states of central Europe that will join Russia as its allies. They are also "the false enemies," i.e. former NATO allies, who will turn out to be very effective in tearing down the "rampart" of Western Europe. The city of Wroclaw is in south-western Poland, the port of Lubeck is on the Baltic Sea, north-east of Hamburg, and Meissen is located a short distance from Dresden, towards Berlin. The catch is, while Wroclaw will be high and dry, Lubeck will definitely be deep below the new sea level, and Meissen, so deep inland, will probably also be inundated. That being the case, the imaginary line connecting these three cities can only indicate a tentative "rampart" separating the two parties in the conflict during the initial stages of The War. The quatrain also implies that the former East Germany will "take the barbarian side," the barbarian being the Russian led alliance.

"Beast wild with hunger will cross the rivers —
the greater part of the battlefield adjacent to Danube.
Into a cage of iron, the great iron thirteenth,
while the child of Germany notices nothing." 2/24

"When the greatest one carries off the prize
of Nuremburg, of Augsburg, and those of Basel,
Frankfurt retaken by the leader of Cologne.
He will cut through Flanders, heading for France." 3/53

"Not from Spain, but ancient France,
will he be elected for the trembling ship.
He will make a promise to the enemy,
who will cause a cruel plague during his reign." 5/49

The "beast wild with hunger" are the starving Russians and their allies, who will entrap the German army in "a cage of iron," made up of tanks, without their command being aware of it. Subsequently, Germany will be turned into "the great iron thirteenth," or the thirteenth member of the red alliance.

The "greatest one," of quatrain 3/53, refers to the Russian leader conquering Germany. Frankfurt will be temporarily relieved, before the Russian-led armies will "cut through Flanders, heading for France." Quatrain 5/49 refers to the French leader of the Western alliance, who will attempt to "make a promise to the enemy," but will obviously fail reaching an agreement, because the Russian-led alliance "will cause a cruel plague." This "plague," as we shall see much more clearly later on, will take the form of nuclear weapons, used in south-western Germany. Nostradamus does not really tells us much about the situation in Germany at that time, but what he does tell us is enough to perceive a nearly total destruction of the Western armies in south-eastern Germany.

However, in his Letter to Henry II Nostradamus tells us of stiff Western resistance in the south-western part of the country, which will end in an extreme tragedy:

> "And this city of Aachen will be surrounded and assailed on all sides by a most powerful force. Their maritime forces will be weakened by the Westerners. And great desolation will fall upon this realm, and its greatest cities will be depopulated and those who enter within will fall under the vengeance of the wrath of God ... Oh, what a calamitous affliction will pregnant women bear at this time."

The first two sentences of the quote above are quite self-explanatory. The rest is clearly describing a fairly massive use of tactical nuclear weapons by the Russians, including the effects of the nuclear fallout on the fetuses, many of whom will likely be born malformed. This quote also confirms the warning about the cruel plague from quatrain 5/49. To make sure we shall not "misunderstand," Nostradamus provides for us further details about the effects of nuclear weapons, and even a hint about their construction.

> "The Sabine tears will no longer be of value:
> Human flesh is burnt alive to ashes ..." 5/16

> "By fire from the sky the city is almost incinerated ..." 2/81

> "Living fire will be let loose, death hidden
> inside dreadful globes. Horrible, frightful." 5/8

Starting with the last sample, we have to acknowledge nuclear devices indeed create "fireballs," when triggered above the target, easily compared to a "living fire," as described in 2/81. This "living fire" is unleashed the moment the two hemispheres of weapon-grade plutonium, or enriched uranium, are driven together inside the nuclear device, and form a complete "globe." Furthermore, Nostradamus used the word "globe" in plural, because he knew that several such devices will be used, and he described the use of these weapons in several localities, including the aforementioned south-western Germany, as well as in southern France, northern Italy, and perhaps even somewhere along the eastern seaboard of the North American continent. He also indicated that at least four fleets of warships will be melted and / or incinerated, and that most of this beastly destruction will be done by the Russians. Also, not surprisingly, he mentions "monsters" being born, most likely resulting from genetic mutation, caused by the irradiation, in quatrains 1/58, 2/32, and possibly 9/32 as well. Equally unsurprising is the fact that large portions of the European continent will become uninhabitable, because of the radiation.

> "The populated lands will become uninhabitable;
> great disagreement over arable land …" 2/95

Such problems will become ever more pronounced, as human stupidity and obstinacy further reduce the land left available after the sea level rise, and the advancing glaciers, by rendering it useless with nuclear weapons.

But to continue with the disheartening news of this War.

As Nostradamus notes in his Letter to Henry II, the Russian-led "maritime forces will be weakened by the Westerners." This probably will occur as a result of a revolt by the recently surrendered and co-opted German navy, that will most likely take a place after the Russians will nuke the German cities.

> "By the victory of treacherous deception
> two fleets are one; then a German revolt …" 6/77

This quatrain harks back to quatrains 2/24 and 3/53, where we have learned of the German defeat, that will take place, thanks to treachery and deception, but still result in the German army and navy becoming a part of the Russian-led alliance.

> "After the combat & naval battle,
> the great Neptune in his highest belfry.
> Red adversary will become pale with fear,
> putting the great Ocean in terror." 3/1

I can only assume that the above quatrain is referring to "the combat and naval battle" for Aachen, located, at that stage, near the new seashore, and it will most likely be after this battle, possibly fought by other Western troops, that the German navy will revolt. The Russians are called here the "red adversary," because they will be behaving with the same ruthlessness as they did during their communist period. And who knows, maybe they will again trade their Russian imperial flag for the red communist one, maybe with twelve, later thirteen yellow stars, to represent their alliance.

The second line is suggesting either an unprecedented storm, or, more likely, an extremely furious naval battle, which will not deliver victory to the Russians. Fearful that they might lose control of the high seas, and possibly lose the war itself, they will resort to an absolute terror, in their future encounters with the Western navy. That most likely means they will attempt to destroy it as fast and as completely as possible.

"The aimless army departs from Europe
to rejoin near the submerged island:
The NATO fleet folds up ..." 2/22

The submerged island is Britain, which will disappear under the sea in the wake of the asteroid's impact. (Re: 9/31) The NATO fleet will presumably carry also what will be left of the retreating Western army, and deposit these on the friendly shores of south-western France. Eventually, after one or more encounters with the Russians, the fleet "folds up." (We should also note here that in the original text NATO was written as an anagram, Arton, or Nator.)

"The naval forces divided in three parts.
Its provisions failing, the second one,
exasperated, seeking the Elysian Fields.
The first one entering the breach will have victory." 9/97

"Naval battle into the night.
The ships on fire, the West is ruined ..." 9/100

Faced with the inevitable, the Western naval forces will be divided into three parts, near the "submerged island." Running out of rockets and ammunition, i.e. the "provisions," one third of the combined fleet will seek "the Elysian Fields." Since the myths have always located them in the westerly direction, the name is virtually synonymous with North America. Another one third, "the first one," will find a "breach" within the ranks of the Russian-led navy and escape, finding a victory at a later date. The remaining one third of the Western fleet will sacrifice itself, and fully provisioned accept the battle. Realizing that "the bird has flown the cage," again, the Russians will be furious.

"The orchestrator of the naval war,
the unbridled red one, severe, with horrible gripe ..." 6/91

This "horrible gripe" will trigger the complete destruction of the remaining one third of the Western navy, as described in quatrain 9/100 above. At that stage, the Russians will also start turning against the civilian population and against their religion.

"Blood of the innocents, of the widow and virgin.
So many evils committed by means of the great Red One.
Holy images placed over burning candle.
Stiff with fear, none will be seen to move." 8/80

Yet, the bloody bulldozer of the Russian-led army will not stop there.

"The dreaded army of the Narbonne's enemy
will greatly terrify the Westerners.
Parpignan vacated with blinding speed,
then Barcelona will send arms by sea." 6/56

"Hard along the great mountains of Pyrenees
a great army will confront the eagle:
Veins cut, forces exterminated.
The (army) chief will chase them as far as Pau." 4/70

"The eagle pushed back around the tents
will be chased there by other birds,
when the sound of the cymbals, trumpets & bells
will restore the senses to the mad lady." 2/44

Just like the previous sample of quatrains, these three also provide us with a more or less continuous story, cut up into a puzzle. It essentially tells us that the Russians will launch a reign of terror in southern Germany and northern France, and that there will be no Western force there to put a stop to it. Then, most likely the same year and the same season, i.e. summer, the Russian-led army will march, (re: 3/53, page 46), virtually unopposed, to southern France, towards Narbonne, near which the largest collection of

French and allied troops will be located, along with the representatives of the government.

However, it is equally possible the Russians will launch a three-pronged attack simultaneously on three fronts: one in south-eastern Germany, one in south-western Germany, and one punching right through the middle, aiming for southern France.

Before we go on though, I would like to point out that, without an exception, the names of the cities on, or near the sea coasts, were again used by Nostradamus for general orientation purposes only, the same way he sometimes uses longitudes, because cities such as Narbonne, Parpignan, Pau, or Barcelona, not to mention all the others, will no longer exist as such, being either inundated, smashed by the tidal waves, or both.

Now, returning to our war scenario, we can say that the available Western forces will be fast retreating southwards, towards the Pyrenees, most likely due to their relatively smaller size, the lack of proper arms and ammunition. These then will reach them, at the twelfth hour, from Spain, conceivably not only by the sea, but also overland, accompanied by sizable units of Spanish army.

Being bled along the way, and tired from lack of food and rest, the Russian-led army will probably enter the foothills of the Pyrenees, and run into well prepared defense positions of the great Western army. Furthermore, Nostradamus also implies that one of the Western ships rescued from the aforementioned naval battle will be one of the small British aircraft carriers. Sailing around the Iberian Peninsula, it will most likely arrive exactly when needed: on an exceptionally calm, sunny day, (for that time period), to help clobber the raiders. Thus the Russian imperial "eagle … will be chased there by other birds." Those 'birds' being the British jets.

The Russian-led troops will not only be "exterminated" on the battlefield itself, their remnants will be driven into the sea, near the town of Pau, to drown there like lemmings. The local population, consisting mainly of refugees from submerged cities, and living largely in tents, (2/44 and 5/76), as well as the Western population at large, will be overjoyed, having escaped the wrath of the enemy, and burst out in celebration.

But more importantly, this new state of affairs "will restore the senses of the mad lady." This "lady" is again none other than Artemis, "madly" hunting down berserk humans. As a result of all this, the Western alliance will sign some kind of a treaty with the Russian-led alliance. Unfortunately, only France, Italy, and Spain will be the remaining partners in the Western alliance by then. It is also indicated that this peace treaty will be facilitated by a new Russian leader.

> "Mars & the scepter will be in conjunction —
> a calamitous war under Cancer.
> A short time afterwards a new king will be anointed
> who, for a long time, will bring peace to earth." 6/24

The first line tells us that war and the intent to rule will dominate the scene. The war will be calamitous, for both sides, and it will take place under the sign of Cancer, or essentially in June and July, which fits our premise perfectly. Since having a peace or war will depend essentially upon the Russians, the "new king" then has to be a new Russian dictator. However ...

> "The two will not remain united for long,
> and within thirteen years under Barbarian Rule.
> There will be such a loss on both sides
> that one will bless the Bark & its leader." 5/78

The two in question are the Russian-led alliance and the French-led alliance. The thirteen years mentioned in the previous quatrain is not, of course, a very long time, but having experienced about four years of horror, thirteen years of peace will probably feel like a long time. After that, most of the French-led alliance will fall under the Barbarian Rule; that is under the Moslem domination, and fairly soon after so will also much of the Russian-led alliance. This later conflict will be so expensive in human lives, that the previous thirteen years will be remembered almost fondly. The "bark" here represents the "united" Europe and its leader, or leaders, because, it would seem, Europe will be a confederation of dictatorships, under the Russian guidance, somewhat like the New Roman Empire under the German emperors.

Unfortunately though, in order to explain the conclusion of hostilities between the two European alliances, we had jumped the timeline quite a bit, and now have to retrace our steps in the required direction.

> "Five partners accuse France of neglect.
> Tunis, Algeria stirred up by the Persians.
> Leon, Seville, and Barcelona fail.
> They will not have the fleet because of the Venetians." 1/73

We are introducing the above quatrain here in order to turn our attention to the coming Moslem presence in the affairs of Europe. In this respect it is fairly unimportant who the five partners are, although we can be pretty sure they include Italy, Spain, Russia, and possibly two junior partners, such as Switzerland and Portugal, or even the British, resettled in France. The next two lines of the same quatrain refer to the first Arab retake of Spain, inspired and most likely coordinated by the Persians, who needed the North Africans to open up a second front in Europe, to help with their invasion of Italy, which most likely was their destination all along. The remnants of the Western navy fighting the Persian invasion are the so called "Venetians," who will fail the Spanish.

There are references in several quatrains to an unspecified foreign presence along the entire northern part of the Adriatic Sea, which would suggest the Persians will invade that part of Europe, after they conquer Greece and Macedonia. Their advance will not stop until they reach the mountainous northern part of Italy. (Re: 2/84 and 6/75)

> "Near the Ticino the inhabitants of the Loire,
> Geronne & Saone, Seine, Tain & Gironde
> will construct a promontory beyond the mountains.
> Conflict engaged in, Po seized, submerged in waters." 6/79

Ticino is a Swiss canton bordering Italy, just north-west of Milan. Promontory is a high ridge of rock jutting into a body of water. However, what Nostradamus has in mind is a wall connecting the lakes di Commo with Maggiore, and most likely extending to the high Alps on the sides of the lakes as well. In a sense a later day version of the Chinese and the Hadrian walls, which were also intended to keep out the barbarians. In this case, the Persians. The attackers will be repelled and driven back to the "river Po." The catch is, the river will no longer be there, because due to the new sea level much of northern Italy, situated less than 100 meters above the current sea level, will become a part of the Adriatic Sea, ending somewhere near Milan. In fact the very last line of the above quatrain tells us that the river Po will be "submerged in waters."

Because of its strategic importance, Nostradamus refers to this defense wall in at least three additional quatrains, 2/25, 3/33, and 4/90, of which we shall quote, at this stage, only the second half of the quatrain 3/33:

"Foreign army—a great country ruined.
The friends will pass through the Walls & the Alps." 3/33

To repel, or at least to stall the Persians, will be obviously of greater importance to the French than helping out the Spanish against the invasion from North Africa. On the other hand, the French will fight and die in Italy, as is attested to by several quatrains. (3/32,38,39, and 43)

"People from around Tarn, Lot & Garonne,
beware crossing the Apennine mountains.
Your tomb is near Rome & Ancona,
the dark-haired man will set up a trophy." 3/43

"The great tomb of the people of Aquitaine
will approach from the direction of Tuscany ..." 3/32

"The Gallic people & the foreign nation
will be killed, captured and wasted beyond the mountains,
in an adverse time & near the harvest time.
By the Lords an accord is drawn up." 3/38

These three quatrains are more or less self-explanatory, within the established context. The only thing that should perhaps be added here is note that "the foreign nation" is the same as "the people of Aquitaine," who are the survivors of the British people transplanted there. Nevertheless, an accord will be reached "by the Lords," that no doubt will include not only the French and Persian Lords, but also the Russian one. This accord will finally enable the French to turn their attention to the situation in Spain, which, in the meantime, will become almost completely occupied by the Arabs, while a large portion of the Spanish army will have retreated to France, along with the leading elements of the Spanish society.

"Because of death, France will undertake a voyage —
fleet by sea, marching over the Pyrenees mountains.
Spain in trouble, soldiers on the march.
Some of the greatest ladies brought to France." 4/2

The above quatrain fits the picture perfectly—once we reverse the sequence of the two lines on the bottom and of the two lines on the top. The word "death" refers to the general state of affairs in Spain at that time. In the Letter to Henry II, we are presented with a similar scenario:

"And a new incursion will be made on the maritime shores
to deliver the fallen Castulum from the first Arab
recapture."

Castulum, a Latin version of Castilla, represents Spain. But more importantly, take a note of the phrase "the first Arab recapture," referring to the first conquest of Spain by the Arabs, early in the 8th century C.E. It also forewarns us to the fact that, after being liberated from the recapture, it will be invaded and captured again.

"The great city of Tarshish by the Gauls
will be destroyed, all in turban captured.
Help from the sea by the great Portugese.
The first day of summer, dedicated to St. Urban." 6/85

The ancient city of Tarshish, or Tarsus, became the modern day Spanish city of Sevilla, in the south of the country. Situated in a lowland near the sea, Sevilla too will be under water, including most likely the Moorish castle of Alhambra, on a hill above it. Again, this must be only a general indication of the location where the final battle that will end the first recapture will take place—on the first day of summer, which nominally falls on June 21st. The only surprising thing in all of this is the fact the Portugese would still have any warships at that stage, and would remain unconquered.

"The two will be contently united together
when, for the most part, the war is binding them.
The African leader trembles in fear.
The bilateral alliance harmed by a fleet." 5/23

"The great Arab marches well to the fore;
he will be betrayed by the Byzantians.
The ancient Rhodes will come to confront him,
and greater harm through other Europeans." 5/47

"After the great affliction of the scepter,
two enemies will be defeated by them.
The African fleet will be launched against the Europeans.
Horrible events on sea & land." 5/48

The three quatrains above sum up the initial stages of the second Arab re-conquest of Europe. The "two," of the quatrain 5/23, most likely refers to the European-Persian accord, of quatrain 3/38, strengthened by the external threat. Most likely the main reason the Russians will agree to it in the first place. Initially, the North Africans will fear this new alliance, and see it as direct threat, and expect to be attacked by it. In the meantime though, events will take place in the Arab world, which Nostradamus does not explain, that will lead to the creation of an awesome Arab / African fleet. It will be this fleet that will severely afflict members of the Russo-French alliance.

According to the quatrain 5/47, this Arab advance will be checked by Persians, the new "Byzantians," who will be, at that stage, an active member of the new accord. The "ancient Rhodes" will also confront the Arabs, as will a number of unspecified European allies. After these initial setbacks to their aspiration to power, "the great affliction of the scepter," the Arabs will eventually defeat the forces of the new accord, the "two enemies." If so, the defeat of the Persians would be only symbolical, or temporary, as we shall see later. To clarify further the phrase "the great affliction of the scepter," it probably also refers to the long outstanding aspiration of the Arabs to be a world power, thwarted by their expulsion from Spain, over 500 years ago, and nearly extinguished by the collapse of the Ottoman (Turkish) Empire, more than 200 years ago.

> "The people of Rhodes demanding relief;
> through neglect her heirs abandoned.
> The Arab empire reveals its own source of relief.
> The West is their route to recovery." 4/39

Quite often "uncertain" translations, copied from book to book, led to rather fuzzy interpretation of the above quatrain. But from the way it now stands, the implications are pretty clear: For the Arabs the "route to recovery," not just from the historical setbacks, but also from the devastation caused by the climatic change, will be the conquest of Europe, starting with Rhodes, abandoned to its fate by the Europeans.

> "France, if you sail into the Ligurian sea,
> you will find yourself besieged among islands & seas,
> opposed by Moslems; more so in the Adriatic.
> You will gnaw the bones of horses & asses." 3/23

Obviously, the seas of the classical world will be thick with Moslem ships, i.e. Arab, as well as Persian, and these will be in position to defeat any naval force the Europeans will be able to muster against them. While Nostradamus does not explain anything about the origin of the Arab fleet, he does tell us about the origin of the mighty Arab armies that will eventually conquer much of the habitable parts of Europe.

"A great host & sect of crusaders
will be raised in Mesopotamia.
From a nearby stream a fickle company
will regard such a rule as hostile." 3/61

"In Arabia Felix
will be born one powerful in the laws of Mahomet,
to vex Spain, conquer Grenada,
and most of the people of Liguria from the sea." 5/55

"For Asia (Minor) a great prohibition.
Also in Mysia, Lycia & Pamphilia.
Blood will flow because of the absolution
of a dark young man filled with evil intentions." 3/60

Starting with the first quatrain of this trio, we are told of a large army being assembled somewhere in northern Iraq, or southern Syria, the land of ancient Mesopotamia. And if Iraq, it will have to be in the northern part , because the south, most likely right up to Baghdad, will be under water, as shall be, for example lower Egypt.

The expression "a nearby stream" probably refers to the river Kelkit, in north-eastern Turkey, whose source is located near the source of the river Tigris, flowing through Iran. As we noted, at that time Turkey, or Asia Minor, will be the seat of the new Persian empire, that will regard such action, on its very doorstep, to be a hostile act. This assumption will, of course, turn out to be correct, and this pan-Arab army will attack the fickle Persians from the rear, as if it were, where they will be most vulnerable.

The third quatrain sketches out for us the subsequent events: "a great prohibition," throughout today's Turkey, against being sympathetic towards the Arab cause, much more so against joining it. Yet, the absolutist, i.e. dictatorial "dark young man" will prevail, after a bloody war that will forge new links between the Arabs and the Persians, who, being both Moslems, will unite against the "infidels."

We shall avoid here all the gruesome details of the next phase of the war. As Nostradamus notes in quatrain 1/15: "Seventy times shall the blood be shed." And by this, I am certain, he means only the major battles of this War of Survival. For example:

> "The inhabitants of Marseilles completely changed.
> Flights and pursuits right up to Lyon.
> Narbonne, Toulouse outraged by Bordeaux.
> Almost a million killed, captured." 1/72

> "One man will proclaim peace for all,
> but in a short while, pillage & rebellion.
> Because of a refusal, town, land & sea ransacked.
> A third of a million dead or captured." 1/92

Again, because of the tsunamis and the risen sea level, there will hardly be anything left of today's Marseilles. Yet, what Nostradamus is telling us is that the greatly reduced French population of the region, and the various Italian and Greek refugees living there, will be displaced by Arab population. The attacking Arabs will pursue the locals all the way to Lyon. During this one specific conflict "almost one million" people will be "killed, captured." In a similar conflict, with the same enemy, described in the subsequent quatrain, "a third of a million" will be killed or captured. The last quatrain most likely also refers to the refusal of the European population to accept their fate, to be "pacified" by the conquerors, which will lead to the consequences outlined here.

> "From the east will come the Punic heart,
> to anger the Adriatic & Romulus' heirs,
> accompanied by the Lybian fleet.
> Maltese temples & nearby islands deserted." 1/9

> "Saturn & Mars in Leo. Spain captured
> by a Lybian chief in a fraudulent conflict ..." 5/14

The "Punic heart" most likely refers to Hannibal, the famous general from Carthage, in today's Tunisia, who set out to defeat Rome on its home ground. Yet, the quatrain 1/9 clearly says these conquerors will come from the east, which would indicate the pan-Arab armies from Iraq and Saudi Arabia, referred to earlier. This massive army, as suggested, will be supported by a North-African fleet, and wreak havoc in the seas surrounding Italy, and within Italy itself. The island of Malta will be deserted, because its population will just get washed away by the tidal waves, and most of its surface will be under water. A similar fate will afflict the "nearby" islands of Sicily, Sardinia and Corsica. But it is also possible that most of these islands will have been repopulated during the previous decade, and then deserted.

The (top half of the) subsequent quatrain reconfirms that Spain will suffer the second recapture by the North Africans, with help from the Saudi Arabians, as stated in 5/55, who in turn will attack from there southern France and northern Italy.

> "From Barcelona such a great army by sea.
> All of Marseilles trembles with fear.
> The islands seized, sea aid cut off.
> Your caretaker is fumbling on land." 3/88

The above quatrain again confirms the assumption we made earlier about the "change of population" of Marseilles. The "sea aid" most likely refers to food shipments from North America, implied in other quatrains as well. The "caretaker" obviously is the government of the day in France.

> "After the victory of the Lion at Lyon,
> a great slaughter among the mountains of Jura.
> Floods & 150,000 Negroes.
> Lyon & Ulm turned into a Mausoleum of death & a tomb." 8/34

The phrase "victorious Lion" probably refers to the remnants of the British troops on French soil. The Jura mountains stretch along the French-Swiss border, located roughly half-way from the Mediterranean coast to the city of Ulm in south-eastern Germany, which, at that stage, will be a part of the Russian alliance. But the main reason for presenting this particular quatrain here is to introduce the evidence of black African Moslems on the battlefields of future Europe, as does the quatrain 4/3: "From Arras & Bourges the Negroes' great banners." At about the same time the Wall and the fortress on the Swiss-Italian border will also fall.

> "The two armies cannot join up at the walls.
> At that moment Milan & Ticino tremble.
> Hunger, thirst & doubt whether the fort will hold out.
> No meat, no bread, no victuals. No one to have a mouthful." 4/90

"The foreign guard will betray the fortress.
Hope & shadow of exceedingly high marriage.
Guard deceived, the fort taken from two sides.
Loire, Saone, Rhone, Garone outraged to death." 2/25

I can only speculate, but "the two armies," both of them Western, "cannot join up," because they are fighting their separate battles on their respective sides of the Wall, with their backs to it, while their supply lines will be severed by the enemy.

The Wall is going to be very long, so it is quite conceivable that one of the guards, possibly of Arab descend, as is about ten percent of the French population, will betray "his" people, while in another place another guard, most likely at the opposite side of the Wall, will be deceived. As a consequence, the Wall will be "taken from two sides," and the Arabs, possibly with a Persian help, will gain a virtually unrestricted access to France from Spain and from Italy. Of course the French will be "outraged to death," because they will know that death is coming.

"The royal bird over the solarian city.
For seven months it will give nightly predictions:
The Wall in the east made expensive–flashes, thunderous noise.
Exactly in seven days the enemies are at the gates." 5/81

The "royal bird" must be an American satellite, monitored from a "solarian" city somewhere in the Midwest, where they would observe, during the night, the war situation taking place in Europe during the day, and inform the Europeans, somehow, of the enemy movements. The battle for the Wall will obviously last for about seven months, and the Western troops will make the victory expensive for the Moslem forces, in terms of human lives, but the final attack will deliver the Wall to the Moslems in only seven days.

However, it will take years for the events to reach the stage described above. As we shall see from the next few quatrains, the French will be able to "check" the Arabs and the Persians for seven years, with some help from their Russian-led allies. Eventually though, France will end up being almost completely devastated, especially in the south.

"Avoid, flee Toulouse, the reds (will)
turn (their) sacrifice into an expiation ..." 9/46

"From the height of the Aventine hill a voice cries:
Leave, leave, all of you on both sides.
The blood of the red ones will appease the anger ..." 9/2

"The Gaul who maintains an empire during the war
will be betrayed by his young brother-in-law ..." 10/34

"Frejus, Antibes, the towns around Nice,
greatly devastated by sea & by land:
the locusts, by land & sea, on favourable wind.
Captured, dead, trussed up, plunder without law of war." 3/82

As Nostradamus tells us, the Russian-led troops, "the reds," will try to make up for the past transgressions with their blood, by attempting to stem the Moslem tide, which the seer compares to "the locusts," but only with a temporary success. On the other hand, the "young brother-in-law," the transplanted British, will betray the French, but the sacrifice "of the red ones" will buy enough time for millions of destitute people to find refuge in North America:

"Infinite people will pass by the sea;
a quarter million will not escape." 2/94

"The bridge of ships will carry millions.
but the bridge is broken by the resistance of the third." 8/21

The "third," in the above quatrain, are the Moslems, who will obviously be barred from participating in this mass evacuation / migration. The "quarter million," who "will not escape," will be from the population selected for the exodus. However, this migration, along with the years of fighting, are going to weaken not only the French-led alliance, but also the Russian-led alliance, and they will no longer be able to block the advance of the Moslem alliance, which most likely will be formed in the defeated France.

"He who attains the kingdom of Navarre,
when Sicily & Naples are allies,
will hold Bigorre & Landes, through Foix & Oloron,
from one too closely allied with Spain." 3/25

"Pretenders enter the fields of the people of Rhone,
where these crusaders will be almost united ..." 8/91

"Libyan prince powerful in Europe;
the French will be seduced by the Arab.
A literary scholar, he will condescend
to translate the Arab language into French." 3/27

These three quatrains trace the evolution of a unified Moslem rule in Europe. The quatrain 3/25 tells us of at least four separate Moslem 'kingdoms': One straddling both sides of the Pyrenees, one in Sicily, one in Naples, and one in Spain. In quatrain 8/91 we encounter the already familiar "crusaders" from Mesopotamia, we have been introduced to in quatrain 3/61. The Libyan prince of the last quatrain is probably the first ruler of the Moslem alliance. Its main goal will be to take over the rest of the habitable parts of Europe, which will mean attacking the Russian-led alliance.

"Near Serbia, in order to assail Hungary.
The herald of Budapest will come to warn them.
The Byzantine chief, Solon of Slovenia,
will come to convert them to the Arab law." 10/62

"Transplanting into the Greater Germany,
Brabant & Flanders, Ghent, Bruges & Bologna.
The truce feigned, the great duke of Armenia
will assault Vienna and Cologne." 5/94

"Through life & death the rule in Hungary will change.
The law will become harsher than serfdom ..." 2/90

"From Danube & the Rhine will come to drink
the Great Camel and will not repent of it.
Those of the Rhone tremble & more still those of the Loire.
Near the Alps the cock will ruin him." 5/68

In the last quatrain, we can hear an echo of the quatrain 8/34, describing a great battle in which the French defeat an army of black Moslems. This, most likely, will be the first attack against the Russian-led alliance, and its failure will lead to the truce, mentioned in quatrain 5/94. Unable to enter though "the front door," the Moslem alliance will enter through the more vulnerable "back door," that is through Hungary, as described in quatrains 10/62, 2/90, and 10/61. This truce-breaking attack will obviously be led by the Persians, situated then in former Yugoslavia, Greece, northern Italy, and throughout the Balkan region.

In the early stages of their future conquest, the Persians will have also absorbed Armenia, and "the great duke of Armenia" will be either an Armenian "convert," or rather a land-title of a Persian overlord. It will be then this duke who will end-up ruling the territories stretching from northern Italy (Bologna), to Hungary, Austria, and virtually all of Greater Germany. Living conditions, as the quatrain 2/90 suggests, will be appalling in all the conquered countries.

> "After the seat was kept for seventeen years,
> five will rule within that period of time.
> At that time one will be elected
> who will not be too conforming to the Europeans." 5/92
>
> "For nine years the thin one will uphold the peace.
> Then he falls for an expensive thirst for blood.
> Because of him a great nation will die without faith or law.
> Killed by a man with a much better character." 2/9
>
> "The younger son will succeed the elder one.
> Much greatness, as far as the reign of privileges.
> His raw glory will be feared by all,
> but his babies will be ejected from the realm." 2/11

The three quatrains above continue the story of The War of Survival, covering a period of some twenty six or twenty seven years, from the point outlined in quatrain 3/27. Towards the end of that period "the thin one," aka "the elder one," possibly unable to deal with the ever worsening problems of food production, due to the ever colder climate, will most likely go berserk, and order the genocide of an entire nation. We can even surmise it will be remnants of the surviving Italians who will be ordered exterminated, in order to have more food for the Arab population, because quatrain 8/54 flatly states that the Spanish will be the second nation to be butchered, most likely during the Arab retreat. "Of the Spanish a second butcher shop is made." The fate of the Greeks, only implied by their absence, will most likely have been already sealed by then.

Fearing repercussions, the "younger brother" gets rid off of "the elder one," but does so a tad too late, because the Americans, horrified by the events in Europe, will finally decide to act.

"For a long time a grey bird will be seen in the sky,
near Dole & the land of Tuscany,
holding a green bough in its beak.
Soon great dying & the war ends." 1/100

This quatrain hints at what we just talked about: the twenty six years of peace, suggested by the perennial "dove of peace," flying, as it were, over north-eastern France and northern Italy. The last line, I suspect, was intended to imply "fast," by the word "soon."

"When the downfall of the lunar ones approaches,
they will not be too distant from each other.
Cold, desiccation, danger around the frontiers —
even where the oracle had its source." 3/4

The "lunar ones" are the Moslems, their fate and their termination directly linked to the termination of the Lunar Age, the Age of the Moon. Located in Spain, France, Italy, southern Germany, Austria, Hungary, and throughout the Balkans, they will indeed "not be too distant from each other." This quatrain also tells us that, at that stage, most of the habitable parts of Europe, due to the quickly advancing ice age, will be getting too cold for permanent habitation, including southern France, where "the oracle", Nostradamus, used to live. In fact by then southern France will be the new climatic frontier. As noted, it will most likely be these climatic conditions that will trigger the genocide. What will follow is outlined, among other such details, in the Nostradamus' Letter to Henry II:

"At this time the third king of Aquilon, hearing the lament
of the people of his principal title, will raise a mighty army
and will pass through the straits of his predecessors
and ancestors, returning it largely to its former state."

Wealth of additional information, dealing with the same subject, can be gleaned from the following quatrains.

"Let weapons and instruments be enclosed in a fish.
Out of it will come men armed for a war.
The fleet will travel far across the sea,
to appear at the Italian shore." 2/5

"The fatal & eternal cycle
will turn in timely order.
The chains of the Phoenician port will be broken,
the city taken and the enemy as well." 3/79

"The great man from a foreign country captured,
in chains of gold offered to Chyren.
Those of Ausonia, Milan, will lose the war,
and his entire army killed by fire & weapons." 4/34

"The remaining blood will not be spilt.
Venice seeks for help to be given.
Having waited a very long time,
the city is liberated after the first trumpet call." 4/1

"Near & far, the failure of two great luminaries,
who will be surviving between April & March.
Oh, what a loss! But two great & kind ones
assisting all parties by land and sea." 3/5

The quote and the five quatrains above provide a more or less continuous story of the initial stages of liberation of Europe, or at least a very brief outline of it.

Now to the details implied. The "third king of Aquilon," that is of the North, is the United States. (The other two "kings" are Western Europe and Russia.) The expression "principle title" could best be rendered as a "principle inheritance" of culture. Of Western, or European culture that is. The "straits of his predecessors and ancestors" is the Strait of Gibraltar. But "returning (Europe) largely to its former state," other than the restoration of basic freedoms and dignity to the population, is another matter. No intervention of any kind will be able to reverse the advancing ice age.

The quatrain 2/5 plainly speaks of a fleet of submarines, aka "fish," filled with soldiers and equipment that will sail into action in Italy, where the aforementioned genocide would be taking place. If it needs pointing out, to carry an army, with all its weapons and adequate supplies, is going to require submarines the size of the proposed submersible oil-tankers, that would have to be designed and built for such a purpose. Also, the expeditionary force is going to need the submarines not only because of the prevalent stormy weather, but also due to the new extent of the Arctic glaciers, and of large break-off icebergs, capable of sinking a regular ship. Furthermore, the use of submarines will be required in order to avoid detection by the Arabs.

The subsequent quatrain 3/79 restates for us that all that will follow has been fated to take place at the specific time. The second half of the quatrain tells us that the defensive "chains" of the "Phoenician port will be broken," and that Moslems will be defeated and / or destroyed, and their leader captured, as we are told in quatrain 4/34, which also confirms the destruction of the local Arab army. This quatrain also reconfirms, in a symbolical fashion, that the Moslem leader will be bound in "chains of gold," that is by the circumstances of the emerging Golden Age, and handed over to "Chyren," which anagram, Cyhern represents the dawning Age of Saturn, that in turn again represents the new Golden Age.

The "Venice" of quatrain 6/1, via the Wends, represents the people of Europe, who all sprung from the Wends. Their cry for help will be heard, and their destruction will be prevented. For the sake of consistency, Nostradamus calls Europe here "the city," but, of course, it is about as much of a city as the St. Augustine's "City of God," which represented the entire world—as well as the state of mind and of culture. Sadly, but no, this "city" will not be "liberated after the first trumpet call." At least not if such a sentence was to be accepted literally, but rather sometimes "after the trumpet call."

As the last quatrain specifically tells us, the process of liberating Europe will start in April, and continue for the entire year, till next March. The first set of the "two great luminaries," are the leaders of the Arab and Persian people, or these peoples themselves, and the "two great and kind ones" are the Americans and their European allies, most likely the Russians, as we shall see shortly.

> "Mars elevated to his highest belfry …
>
> … Those of the Eagle included under the Balance." 5/42
>
> "Victory appears within a year for the Sun & the Eagle.
> Vague assurances provided to the vanquished.
> Neither bugle nor cries will restrain or stop (the slaughter),
> when vengeful peace is being attained hourly through death." 1/38
>
> "Later will come from a distant country
> a Germanic prince upon the golden throne.
> The servitude & the waters are reconciled.
> The lady's service, her times, less than appealing." 2/87

"A German heart born of the Trojan blood
will rise to great power.
He will chase out the foreign Arab people,
returning the Church to its pristine pre-eminence." 5/74

"Like a griffin will come the King of Europe,
accompanied by those of the North.
The reds & the whites will set up a great trap.
(Then) they will march against the king of Babylon." 10/86

"And when the lords of the North, two in number, will be victorious over the easterners, the east will tremble in terror of these Northern brothers, yet not brothers." Letter to Henry II

"When those of the northern polar region are united
the Orient will be in great fear & dread.
A new thrust, facilitated by the great fear:
Rhodes & Byzantium to be stained by Barbarian blood." 6/21

These six quatrains, and the one quote from the Letter to Henry II, tell us a yet another part of the future history. The first and the last line of the topmost quatrain inform us that this conflict will be furious, and of utmost importance, and that "Mars" will be knocking down some historical, as well as mental walls. It also tells us that the Russians, represented here by their imperial eagle, will, once again, become American allies.

Quatrain 1/38 confirms that the Americans, this time as the Sun, the symbol of the coming age, and the Russians, will be victorious within one year. (Re: 3/5) The rest of the quatrain is quite self-explanatory. Then, according to quatrain 2/87, arrives the "Germanic prince," most likely from his North American exile, to sit "upon the golden throne." This constitutes a yet another reference to the coming "Golden Age," or the "Age of the Sun." Under his guidance the people of Europe will reconcile their experiences of the recent servitude, and the consequences of the "waters" of the Flood, with the requirements placed upon mankind's evolution by the Supreme Being. The "lady" in question is Artemis, the defense aspect of Gaia, whose rule time "service" will certainly be found "less than appealing," by all those afflicted by it. However, to speak of the peoples situation as "servitude" is overstating the case, unless servitude to cause is meant. After all, even the planet, that she also represents, will have to perform as she is destined to perform.

Quatrain 5/74 is again addressing the subject of the Germanic prince. The reference to "the Trojan blood" is probably evoking the ability of the Trojans to be on friendly terms with the gods deciding mankind's fate. Ancient Romans believed their city and their civilization was founded by the refugees from Troy, and the French that their royal lineage is descended from the rulers of Troy. The middle two lines are self-explanatory. The "pristine pre-eminence" of the last line probably refers to a spiritual purity alien to any historical Church, and the one Nostradamus most likely has in mind here predates all of them, going back to the forgotten source of spiritual knowledge from which all religions and prophecies sprung.

The "King of Europe," of quatrain 10/86, will probably turn out to be the Germanic prince, after a formal promotion, combining within his ranks "the reds & the whites," the "reds" being the Russians and their original allies, and the "whites" mainly the Germans and the French, along with the other surviving Westerners, allied with the Americans. The rest of the quatrain is again self-explanatory, even if it is somewhat getting ahead of our story line.

The quote from the Letter to Henry II also mentions the same two allies, i.e. the European and the North American forces, and hints at their distant relationship by blood. Byzantium, of the last quatrain, is today's Turkey, and the future seat of the Persian Empire, situated on the future route to the "Babylon," or rather to as yet unspecified destination in the Middle East.

"Twice the high and mighty, twice cast down,
the East will also weaken Europe.
After several battles its adversary (will be)
chased towards the sea & inevitable failure." 8/59

"With great fury will the European King (from Belgium)
wish to wax the barbarian army.
With grinding fury he will chase the Arabs
from Europe to Gibraltar." 5/13

"At a nearby place, not far from Europe,
the two giants from Asia & Africa,
came from Rhine & Danube, they claimed as their Europe.
Cries and tears at Malta, along the Ligurian coast." 4/68

The Third Antichrist will be annihilated very soon.
Twenty seven years will his bloody war last.
The heretics (are) dead, captured, exiled.
Human bodies, blood like water covering frozen earth." 8/77

"The king enters Foix, wearing a blue turban.
He will reign less than a revolution of Saturn.
The king in white turban, his heart dedicated to Byzantium.
Sun, Mars & Mercury near Aquarius." 9/73

"Libra will be seen to reign in the West,
holding the rule over the skies & the earth.
No one will see the might of Asia destroyed,
until the seven will not rule in succession." 4/50

The six quatrains above describe the end of the Moslem rule in Europe, and the last three even tell us how long that rule will last.

The first one from the top informs us, again, that the Moslems will be twice victorious, as well as twice defeated, and that the second defeat will require several fierce battles.

The following quatrain most likely is referring to the same "Germanic prince ... born of the Trojan blood." Since the Belgians blend within themselves the Germanic and the French qualities, such definition would make sense.

The third quatrain speaks of the defeated Moslems, from Asia and Africa, fleeing from central Europe to an African location, while other Moslems, left behind in northern Italy, and elsewhere on the northern shores of the Mediterranean, are lamenting their fate there.

The Third Antichrist, of quatrain 8/77, are the Moslems, in general. (The First Antichrist were the Russian communists, under Lenin and Stalin, as stated by Nostradamus in the Letter to Henry II. The Second Antichrist, while unnamed by him, directly, as far as I know, possibly was Hitler and his cohorts, but we could point the finger at the industrial establishment, or the Russians and their allies. After all, Nostradamus did in the Letter.)

The time period of twenty seven years indicates the duration of the direct Moslem rule in Europe. While stated outright in quatrain 8/77, it can also be arrived at by adding up the years given in quatrains 5/92 and 2/9, plus the one year required to liberate Europe.

The king who will enter Foix, "wearing a blue turban," will in fact be the Arab king of Navarre. "He will reign less than a revolution of Saturn," which takes 29.5 years. Now, if we take the period of twenty seven years as a base for the duration of his rule, and add to it roughly a year, which will be required to drive the Moslems "from Europe to Gibraltar," the resultant figure for the rule of that king will indeed be some two years shy of 29.5 years.

The "king in white turban, his heart dedicated to Byzantium," describes the Persians. We should be familiar, by now, with the symbology of the last line, which can be rendered as: Age of the Sun, War, Transformation—near the beginning of the Age of Aquarius. Although the Age of Aquarius has already started some years ago, the global Flood will make it "official."

The Libra of the last quatrain represents the U.S., via the scales of "blind" justice, being supreme in the future conflict on land and in the air. The seven Moslem rulers of quatrain 4/50 in fact are indicated for us in quatrains 5/92, 2/9, and 2/11, quoted earlier. The last line of quatrain 2/11, that introduced the seventh ruler, states explicitly: "His babies will be ejected from the realm," and their father most likely captured, according to quatrain 4/34.

> "The people of Romania, Angloterritory & Poland,
> and of Bosnia, will form a new alliance,
> in order to pass beyond Gibraltar.
> The Barcelonans & the Tyrrens cruelly finish them off." 5/51

> "The Church of God will be persecuted,
> and the sacred temples will be plundered.
> The child will put own mother out, naked, in a slip.
> The Arabs will ally with the Poles." 5/73

In quatrain 5/51 Nostradamus tells us that the traitors to the European cause will be treated just as ruthlessly as the Moslems. The nations that will sell out completely, for reasons whose only commonality will be physical survival, except perhaps for the Bosnians, will also include the British, resettled in south-western France, called elsewhere "the Aquatines." (Re: 10/34) The only question mark remains about "the Barcelonans & the Tyrrens," because it is highly unlikely there will be enough population left alive in Spain, much less so of military age and capabilities, to mount such an operation—unless Nostradamus had a population newly resettled there from the north in mind. The Tyrhenian Sea, from which the expression "Tyrrens" is usually assumed was derived, includes the islands of Corsica, Sardinia, and Sicily. But these, as we know from other quatrains, will be long void of their indigenous population, unless, again, newly resettled. Perhaps more appropriate meaning of that word, and of the entire expression, could possibly be found in the Norse mythology, and its god of war Tyrr. In this respect the "Tyrrens" would be the "gods" of war, and the Germans the executors of their will.

The quatrain 5/73 actually seems to be describing the conditions under which the Poles will feel compelled to join the Arabs. The first two lines illustrate the future persecution of the Catholic Church in Poland by the Russians. The third line, I suspect, is essentially an allegory. To understand it, one has to know that the Slavic population was forced to migrate eastwards by the invading Germanic tribes, some 2,000 years ago. In this respect, Russia is the "child" of Poland, and it will be this "child" that will most likely exclude its hated "mother" not only from joining the alliance, and from participating in its food-sharing program, but also prevent them from migrating south, sentencing the entire nation in fact to death by starvation and cold, since Poland will be fully exposed to the advancing ice age and its conditions. Perhaps reason enought to join the Moslems.

"At port Selin the tyrant is put to death,
but liberty is not recovered yet.
A new war starts, of vengeance & remorse.
The lady is honored through force of terror." 1/94

The "port Selin" could be any Moslem port, as that word, via the ancient Greek "Selen," refers to the crescent Moon on Moslem flags. The second line speaks not only of the personal liberty, taken away by the foe, but also of the liberty of mind, shackled by the hate and desire for vengeance, generated by the cruelty and horrors suffered, by the remorse over the wasted and destroyed lives. The "lady" in question is again Artemis, the "huntress of men," who is also Kali, the devouring goddess of the Age.

"The Arab prince, War, Sun, Europe, Lion.
The rule of the Church will succumb to the sea.
Towards Persia almost a million men (army).
This serpent will inundate Byzantium & Egypt." 5/25

The first line represents condensed symbolical shorthand. It says a war will be forced upon a Moslem leader that will be fought under the auspices of the Age of the Sun, in which Europe will fight like a fierce lion. The "sea" of the second line refers to the new religion of the sea, but most likely focused on the phenomenon of the ice age, which we shall discuss in one of the subsequent chapters. The bottom two lines are quite self-explanatory, accepting the "serpent" is the column of the European army.

> "Hercules approaches the great Byzantium.
> The barbarian league will be driven out.
> Of the two laws, the pagan one will be expelled.
> Barbarian & freemen in perpetual struggle." 5/80

L'Omigon, the name used by Nostradamus, is Ogmios, the Celtic Hercules. But any Hercules, by any name, in any setting, embodies a wholesale cultural changeover. The rest, again, is quite plain and straightforward.

> "A new law will occupy a new land
> around Syria, Judea & Palestine.
> The great barbarian empire will crumble
> before the (first) century of the Sun is over." 3/97

With the advancing ice age a "new land," or rather the old land, submerged for decades by the sea, will re-emerge. As strange as it might seem to some, we have already entered the Age of the Sun, perhaps some fifty years ago. Even Nostradamus seems to agree with this. For example, in quatrain 9/44 he states: "Saturn will change from gold to iron ..." Here both Saturn and the gold stand for the Age of the Sun that will be temporarily "suspended," or "interrupted," by the impact of the asteroid and by the subsequent wars, symbolized by the "iron" of the past age.

The Moslems will be expelled from Europe about 45 years after the impact. It means that the total destruction of their empire should take place within the subsequent period of five to ten years. In fact Nostradamus, in the Letter to Henry II states: "And the renewal of the triumvirate will last seven years." In the broader context, the "triumvirate" is represented by the three victorious parties to the conflict: The Americans, the Germans and the Russians.

> "On the (battle)fields of Persia, Arabia & Armenia,
> two armies will assemble three times.
> A camp near the banks of Aras.
> The great Suleiman is entombed by earth." 3/31

"The year that the brothers of the lily come of age,
one of them will rule greater Europe.
The mountains tremble, the Latin passage is opened.
Chewing up (the enemy), alliance marches against the Armenian fort." 5/50

"The fortress of the besieged surrounded,
by explosives & fire sunk into a deep abyss.
The instigators all quickly sealed there.
Never did the gravediggers came to such a
pitiful split." 4/40

The three quatrains above focus on the strategic defeat(s) of the Moslem forces, in the countries named in the first line, and the destruction of their command post, deep within the Caucasus mountains in Armenia.

The expression Nostradamus used for Persia was Media, which is situated in the north-western part of today's Iran, next to Armenia, from which it is separated by river Aras, formally known as Araxes. The first of the final three battles will most likely take place there. The second battle will probably take place in Armenia, and it will decide the fate of an underground fort there, yet to be built, within which the Moslem leadership, "the great Suleiman," will be entombed alive. The quatrain 4/40 provides us with some details of that operation. The word "sextons," found in the last line of the original, I translate here as "gravediggers," because that used to be one service performed by sextons, and it seems more appropriate in this context. The expression "pitiful split" refers to the huge chasm, found some years ago by Soviet geologists inside the mountains of the Armenian Caucasus, which they said was virtually "bottomless," and which, in all probability, will be chosen for the site of this future fortress, that will become their grave.

The third and final battle, that is to take place somewhere in the Arabian Peninsula, will essentially be a "mop-up" operation, during which the remaining Moslem forces will be completely destroyed.

"Barbarian empire usurped by the third:
Greater part of its people being put to death.
By him quarter people stricken by a senile death —
through fear that the race might die out." 3/59

The Moslem empire will have consisted, during its European phase, of three peoples: the Arabs, the Persians, and the Europeans, but will be eventually taken over the third group—the Europeans. At that stage The War will be over for good, and most of the Arab and Persian population will be dead, but of those still alive a quarter will succumb to the fear that the entire race is doomed to die. That, however, will not turn out to be the case.

> "Never again will the great one be in a false sleep.
> Eagerness will take the place of slumbering.
> Do raise up the phalanx of gold, blue & vermilion,
> subjugate Africa, gnaw it down on the march." 5/69

The "great one" here is the mankind at large, which he predicted was bound to wake up from its millennia long "false sleep," its mental stupor. The "phalanx of gold" refers to the newly awakened West Europeans, the "blue" are the Arabs, and the vermilion would suggest the Russians and their allies. This multicolored phalanx will set out to subjugate Africa, and to make it its new home.

However, the Arabs who will become a part of this phalanx will most likely be only the children, brought up "Western style," as Nostradamus implies in his Letter to Henry II:

> "And hereupon the principal eastern chief will be afflicted, most of his people vanquished and put to death…and his children imprisoned. And then will be accomplished the prophecy of the Royal Prophet."

Indeed, a prediction exclusively for our near future. After all, the prophet expressly states that his predictions reach no further. He even repeats this promise in quatrain 1/48.

EXTINCTION

Nostradamus complains in his Letter to Henry II: "... most of the prophetic quatrains announce events so harsh that it is impossible to render the means for their interpretation."

First of all, we have to pause at the word "most," because, after naming two dates close to his time, the master states in the following paragraph: "... most of the events ... are going to the events which will take place at the beginning of the seventh millenary ..." This, obviously, is a direct reference to the counting of time, as derived from the events in the Bible. According to this count, the world was "created" in 4,004 B.C.E., which means the seventh millennium nominally started in 2005 C.E. And since, according to the information available in the quatrains and in certain hints in the Bible, The War is to start 3 ½ years after the asteroid impact, and since it is supposed to last a total of some fifty years, we can also conclude that most of the quatrains refer to that specific period, which confirms and exceeds my original estimate.

We also have to agree with Nostradamus that, from the point of view of the historical man, the announced events, their underlying facts, are extremely harsh, since they reveal a mass extinction process, during which entire nations, even races, currently populating the planet, will vanish. Yet, while the fact itself is shocking, we ought to know such fate befell many branches of mankind in the "prehistoric" past. For example, an Asian "myth" informs us that three entire races of people perished during the upheavals that terminated the last Ice Age.

We get an indication of such extinction, through warfare, in the Indian epic of *Mahabharata*, which story also suggests the use of rockets and energy or nuclear weapons. However, by applying today's means of understanding, it is quite possible to interpret sensibly the real cause of such events.

Again, we have to pause for a while, to take stock of what was said, to realize that here private fancies, or fantasies, have to be separated from the super-objective realities, which are all a part of the ongoing evolutionary processes that we will talk more of later on. Right now, however, we have to concentrate on the painful problem at hand; the problem of extinction that will affect directly members of the existent human species.

We have become used, by now, to the notion of extinction, or near extinction, of other animal species, or of small groups of "primitive" native populations. However, Nostradamus predicts that several major branches of mankind will become extinct. Understandably, since he had lived most of his life in southern France, he concentrated his attention on the fate of the regions and countries closest to his domicile and on Europe in general:

> "The seven branches will be reduced to three.
> The elder ones will be surprised by death.
> Two will be seduced into a fratricide,
> The instigators will be in a dormant state." 6/11

The "seven branches" are the seven major European linguistic and cultural groups: Greeks, Italians, Spanish, French, English, Germans and Slavs. The identity of the nations "selected" for the extinction can be derived, among others, from quatrain 8/77, where the prophet states in the first line: "The antichrist very soon annihilates the three ..." Judging from numerous quatrains, "the three" will include the population of Greece, Italy and Spain. The fourth branch to be eliminated from the European family is the British one. The remaining three branches then will include the Slavs, by far the largest linguistic group in Europe, the Germanic people, representing the second largest linguistic group on that continent, and the remnant of the French people.

The destruction of the people is going to have, on the physical plain, four main causes: floods, plagues, starvation, and The War. To repeat the two most striking and relevant quotes: "... France is deserted: Bodies dead by water, brought to the shores, Waiting in vain for the chance to be buried." (4/20) "By flood & mighty plague

The great city is assailed for a long time …" (9/82)

This situation, which would be repeated all around the world, offers only one conclusion: the floods and plagues are directly connected, in a fashion similar to the many plagues that ravished medieval Europe and the world. While most of them were spread by air born viruses, a great many people died of typhoid, also termed a plague back then, caused by "unsanitary conditions," that is by seepage of human feces into the wells from which people drew their water to drink and to cook with. In the near future, with millions of refugees living in similarly unsanitary conditions, these problems are bound to arise again.

In the Letter to Henry II we can also read these words: "… such a plague will arise that of the three parts of the world more than two will perish …" When we add to these losses the ones caused by the Flood, exposure and starvation, we can assume that the global population of some seven and half billion people, at the time of the impact, will be reduced to about two billion. And then The War will start in earnest, as will all the other wars elsewhere, their consequences compounded by cold and starvation.

Nostradamus lists for us, in numerous quatrains, destruction and slaughter on a scale so vast, only the term extinction seems to apply.

> "Leaderless people of Spain & Italy,
> dead and overcome in their peninsulas …" 3/68

> "From Monaco as far as Sicily,
> all the coast will remain deserted …" 2/4

> "The huge grave for the French people
> approaches from the direction of Italy,
> when war will near the German corner,
> and the Italians are being terrorized." 3/32

> "Because of death, it is too late to revive the great nation." 2/45

Yet, in spite of the severity of these outlined events, we have to keep in mind that none of them will be taking place by chance, or merely by human design, and to judge them by human standards would be pointless.

> "The year of the great cycle of the seventh number
> will deliver the times of the Games of Slaughter,
> not far from the age of the great millennium …" 10/74

The very wording, "the Games of Slaughter," suggests a (long) prearranged date for such a bloody "game," where only those "best fit" will survive. However, the evolutionary requirements specified for our survival by the Supreme Being are totally unlike those of social Darwinism. And Nostradamus spelled it out pretty clearly in his Letter to Henry II, that it will be those on the top of the social ladder who will be exterminated by the infuriated mob, while the middle class will fall into decadence.

> "The first one throughout Europe and most of Africa
> will be exterminated by the third one, making use of
> the poor in spirit … And of the three sects, that which is
> in the middle, will be thrown a bit into decadence,
> because of its partisans." Letter to Henry II

The "first one" is the current plutocracy, which is perceived as representing the top social tier. Their elimination in Europe and Africa could be contributable to the delayed ecological backlash, but also to the historical class tensions in Europe. However, class conflicts are bound to flare up everywhere around the world, which became conditioned to the perceived egalitarianism of democracy, wherever the basic physical survival will be threatened by the demands of the privileged few.

> "The great famine, which I sense approaching,
> will often turn (back), then become universal.
> It will be so great and long lasting people will wonder,
> searching for roots, letting babies starve." 1/67

During the onset of this great famine the plutocrats will, as they always have, use their personal resources and privileged positions to buy up as much available food as possible, driving the cost of the remaining supplies out of the reach of ordinary people, thus worsening the famine, as they have always done, during such times. Eventually, and perhaps with some prodding, the mob will turn against the rich with extreme vengeance.

Repeatedly, Nostradamus talks of hecatombs and of extermination, and repeatedly he dates the period of such events.

> "After great misery for mankind, an even greater one approaches,
> when the great cycle of centuries is renewed:
> Rain, blood, milk, famine, war & pestilence.
> In the sky fire will be seen, pulling a long train of sparks." 2/46

"Mabus will soon die, then
a dreadful destruction of people & animals:
Suddenly a vengeance will come to rule,
thirst, hunger, hundred times stronger when the comet comes." 2/62

I strongly suspect that the original title for Nostradamus prophecies, The Centuries, alluded to contents of the quatrain 2/46, which generalizes the events to come, including the all important appearance of the asteroid.

"Leave, everyone leave Geneva,
Saturn will change from gold to iron.
Those against RAYPOZ will be all exterminated.
Before the onslaught the sky shows signs." 9/44

To keep the interpreters guessing, Nostradamus invented a score of anagrams for Saturn. Raypoz (Zaypor) is one of them, as is the Mabus (Sabum) of quatrain 2/62. The rest of the above quatrain, within the established context, is again quite self-explanatory. Yet, it would seem, that the third line was meant to have a general, or global application. The last line, once more, is referring to the asteroid.

EXODUS FROM EUROPE

For this short chapter I have tried to select quatrains that describe the situation in Europe after The War, separating these from the ones I used in the previous two chapters. Whether I have completely succeeded is another matter though, because even during The War large bodies of people will be on the run, either from the floods, from the invading armies, from the ice age climate, or nuclear devastation.

Yet, I will make one purposeful exception here, to round out the perception of the times to come. It concerns the virtual depopulation of Greece, whose people, faced with the Persian onslaught, will try to flee further west, as referred to, obliquely, in quatrain 9/75.

> "From Ambracia & from Thracia,
> people by sea. Evil & aid from the French ..." 9/75

Ambracia, or modern Arta, is a province in western Greece. During the ancient times Thracia included modern day Bulgaria and northern Greece. This suggests people from all over Greece will be fleeing in a westward direction. Perhaps understandably, such a huge influx of refugees would cause serious problems in France, where accommodation would be all but non-existent and food scarce. Also, some of these refugees, such as the Bulgarians, would be less welcome than others, being of non-European, Turkish origin.

> "From Sens, from Autun they will come to Rhone,
> to march beside it towards the Pyrenees mountains.
> The people leaving the Marches of Ancona
> will follow the great routes over land & sea." 2/74

This quatrain provides us with a snapshot of two large bodies of refugees. One surging from northern France, heading for Spain, and the other escaping north-western Italy, heading possibly also for Spain, via France—provided the two events are indeed concurrent, or that they will not happen during the beginning of The War. If that were the case, then the French will be fleeing from the Russian-led invasion from the north, while the Italians will be fleeing the Persian invasion. But another possible interpretation presents itself in the following quatrain 3/8.

We have cited several relevant quatrains in the previous chapters, describing massive shifts of population in the future war-torn Europe, and there is no need to repeat them here. In this chapter I would like to bring your attention to the mass migrations and changeover of the populations in Europe that will occur as The War ends.

> "The Cimbrians, joined by their neighbours,
> will depopulate most of Spain.
> People gathered in Guine & Limousin
> will form a league & join their company." 3/8

The Cimbrians used to be a northern Germanic tribe whose identity vanished about 2,000 years ago. The key indicator here is most likely the word "Germanic," along with the subtle reference to the loss of separate identity to be experienced by "their neighbours," who will become absorbed within the larger body of the Germanic people migrating south, to escape the ice age conditions in their former homelands. The "league" that will be joining the migrating Germans in France, judging from the name-places provided by Nostradamus, could include many ethnic Swiss, or even Austrians, as well as French, since the localities in question are located in northern and central France. In fact Guine is located near Sens and Autun, we remember from quatrain 2/74, which could mean these two quatrains might be connected. But then, the proximity of these two sites could be a mere coincidence. If that were to be the case, the destination of the migrating Italians would remain open to speculation. On the other hand, if the two events were indeed concurrent, as the quatrain 2/74 seems to suggest, it would also mean that a noticeable portion of the Italian population will be saved from the aforementioned Moslem genocide. By the same token, the second half of the said quatrain could also be referring to a fleeing Arab, or Persian population, resettled in Italy. But so could the first half, really. On reflection, the last interpretation seems to be the most likely one.

> "Crossing the bridges to come closer to Rosiers,
> arriving late, yet sooner than imagined,
> the new Spaniards will come to Beziers.
> Thus this chase will shatter the enterprise." 9/25

The above quatrain continues the story of the previous one. The "new Spaniards" are the Germanic people and their allies, possibly also referred to in quatrain 5/13. In spite their haste, re: "this chase," they will be "arriving late" to prevent the butchering of the Spanish people by the Arabs. Yet, their arrival will prevent the completion of this ghoulish enterprise, it "will shatter the enterprise" of genocide. By arriving "sooner than imagined," Nostradamus is saying that only a year before the North American intervention, these Germanic people will greatly fear such a migration will take place much later, further reducing the chances of survival for many of them.

At the same time, as the Germanic people and their allies will be migrating to Spain, the Russians and the remnant of the French population, along with their allies, will be headed for Italy, to pass through it on their way to Sicily, and the other Mediterranean islands, because even Italy itself will be too cold to sustain a civilization.

> "The Albanians will cross into Rome.
> By means of Langres the mob is provisioned.
> The Marquis & the Duke will spare no man.
> Fire, blood, smallpox, no water, the crops fail." 4/98

> "The great Celt will enter Rome,
> leading the masses of exiled & banished ..." 6/28

> "The exiles will come to Sicily,
> to deliver the foreign people from hunger.
> At daybreak the Celts will fail them.
> Life remains by reason; the king joins in." 2/71

The town of Langres is situated somewhat southeast of Paris, and a possible future site of food storage facilities for the defeated Moslem alliance. It will then feed the migrating "mob" of the French, exiled by the climatic conditions from their country.

Encountering the Albanians in Rome, who will have almost certainly become willing members of the Moslem alliance, being of the same faith, the French "will spare no man," i.e. no Albanian. Perhaps the French will try to settle there, but after "the crops fail," because it will be too cold and too dry, they will have to move on further south, to Sicily, where they will "deliver the foreign people from hunger." This, not so cryptic sentence, tells us two things: 1. the foreign people are Arabs, and 2. the "delivery" will take a form of slaughter—"at daybreak." The explanation for this interpretation is found in the last line: Those Arabs who will survive will cling to life only by reason alone. Whether the reason will consist of hopes of revenge, or just of maintaining the race, remains unanswered.

However, the exodus of the Celtic people will not end in Sicily. Even if the conditions were hospitable enough to remain there, which does not seem the case, since we are told the Arabs will be starving there, they would end up isolated from the main body of the European population. In my opinion, the French and their allies will join the Russians and their allies in their march on Africa, we recounted on the last page of the chapter The War of Survival. It would seem that even the Germanic people and their allies will participate in the march on the Middle East and the conquest of Africa, and that Europe is bound to become an empty continent. Nostradamus confirms this much in two separate quatrains:

> "The world approaches its final period.
> Saturn, again, will be late returning.
> Transplanted empire empties out the Black nation ..." 3/92

> "... the people of Europe will hold all of Africa,
> then Saturn occupies their kingdom no longer ..." 5/11

The very last line above simply tells us that Saturn cannot be occupying the European "kingdom," because, being in Africa, it is no longer there. But Saturn will certainly be occupying their new "kingdom" in Africa, obliged to move there with his subjects. The last line of quatrain 3/92 tells us that the Europeans will empty the African continent of its black population, without specifying the means.

EVOLUTIONARY DIVIDE

Principal flaw in Darwinian theory prevented our society from perceiving a few major facts: A) The evolutionary process is guided by the Supreme Being. B) Our evolution, while constantly speeding up, is still ongoing. C) Our evolution and existence has a goal and a purpose, which is also the reason why our species was the last one to evolve.

To demonstrate, however briefly: Homo erectus had been around for over one million years, while our kind, Homo sapiens, has been around for perhaps some 300,000 to 400,000 years. Even within our own species changes did take place, on the order of tens of thousands of years, but these changes remained confined to the size and the shape of our cranium, and these changes, it would appear, did take place in step with climatic changes. For example, during the Ice Age, the average cranium of the so called Cro-Magnons contained circa 30 percent more brain matter, and about 50 percent more neural connection, than does the cranium of the average person living today. The craniums of our species "shrunk," between 11,700 and 10,200 years ago, as the planet substantially warmed up and the "modern" population ended up with a fairly small dolichocephalic, or "boat shaped" skulls. Then, about 4,000 years ago, the brachycephalic, or wide skulled people, with 'bulging' foreheads, started to appear among the general population, again contradicting the current evolutionary theory. During the Little Ice Age, accompanied by plagues and wars, the people with the brachycephalic skulls, from a minority, became the majority in Europe, within a few centuries. Considering that anticipatory, future related and creative centers of the brain are located in the forward situated lobes, such a "redesign" is of a crucial importance. Conceivably, the future upheavals will virtually eliminate all the dolichocephalic people, because the past upheavals served essentially the same purpose.

There are strong hints that Nostradamus was somehow aware of such processes we call evolution, but I am not at all certain he quite understood their importance and significance.

> "... suddenly the time of change approaches,
> neither for a good, nor evil purpose." 3/46

While "neither for good, nor evil purpose" is possibly suggesting something about the objectivity of the forces involved, he obviously failed to comprehend that there are limits to the course of action the Supreme Being, who can only act through nature, may take, and that the primary objective of such corrective actions is the maintenance and preservation of life itself, before anything else.

> "That which is without life & without the ancient sense
> will injure itself mortally through artifice ..." 1/22

You might be surprised, perhaps, but the first line of the above quoted quatrain refers to the human beings in general, and the second line to the technological trap we have constructed for ourselves, especially by the chemicalization of our environment. To put things in a better perspective, we will start out with some comments relating to the second line.

Artifice, obviously, is something unnatural, man-made. While the greenhouse effect is being produced essentially by human activities, and while its consequences will be very serious, causing a lot of suffering and deaths, this affliction at least has a fairly simple cause: excessive emissions of carbon dioxide. However, the quatrain refers to more subtle and more lethal dangers. The sentence "will injure itself mortally" suggests a direct threat to the human viability, to our very ability to survive, brought about "through artifice." The most potent candidate for such role is the soup of chemicals found in numerous products, many of them intended for the households, or directly released into the environment, which then end up in the air we breathe, the water we drink, the food we eat, because many of these chemicals can alter, damage our DNA, or make us infertile. And not just us, but most mammalian species as well. In consequence, mass extinction is a real possibility. So far, as the European and North American studies show, the male sperm count has fallen by some 50 percent during the last generation alone. The prospects of failed genetic and nanotechnological "experiments" would represent an even greater threat in the future.

Concerning the top line of the quoted part of quatrain 1/22 we can say the following: As a universal, unspecialized species, our survival directly depends on our mental capacity, on our ability to concentrate on the crucial problems. Yet indications from many sources suggest that the minds of the youngest generation are already being adversely affected by the chemicals in our environment. The most blatant example is the lead, used as an additive in gasoline, paints, plastics, etc. The rising global temperature is also beginning to affect negatively minds of the youngest generation, just as it did well over 10,000 years ago.

To further demonstrate the point, we have to take a short detour here, through a very abbreviated "history" of Life / Evolution / Universe, which are in fact synonyms for the same phenomenon. The Universe, as far as the quantum mechanics theories are concerned, is a living, thinking entity, acting towards a goal. Also, once we clear up the scientific verbiage surrounding the "peculiar" behaviour of the quantum particles, we realize the Universe is Omnipresent, Omniscient, and even Omnipotent—within the confines of Its own laws.

Those of you who became acquainted with the evolution of the Universe are aware that, from the very beginning, It had to overcome, again and again, mathematically impossible odds, first against Its very physical existence, later against the existence of Life. Since nothing of evolutionary importance happens by chance in this Universe, the appearance of non-specialized, i.e. human species, did not happen by chance either, but is a part of the overall design to maintain Life on this planet. Of course, the evolution of such tool making, thinking beings, would inevitably contain a series of serious hazards to the Life this species was to learn to protect, but these were obviously foreseen, and their outcome was never in doubt.

In this respect, "the universe is unfolding as it should" be unfolding, and ultimately we do not have to worry about the survival of the human species as such, or of the Life at large. A fact that has been known in the ancient times, but lately forgotten, which brings us back again to the first line of the quatrain 1/22, stating:

"That which is without life & without the ancient sense." Obviously, we are not quite without life, but having lost some 50 percent of our neural connections, starting about 11,700 years ago, which was the beginning of the so called Moon Age, mankind lost its higher mental and spiritual capacities. This fact is readily portrayed by all the major mythological systems, and was accepted as fact during the classical times. Even the intellectual elites of the Medieval times, including Nostradamus, were still aware of it. (A Persian "myth" makes an outright claim that mankind lost 99 percent of its mental capacity. More on that subject in my book *Ancient Ecologists*.)

The ancient people used to compare the current mental state of mankind to a "sleep," and every major culture echoes the pointless cry: "Sleeper awake," emulated by Jesus as well, during his envisioned night vigil at the Gethsemane garden, where all his followers present there fell asleep. Jesus then admonishes them: "So, you *men* could not keep watch with me ..." This sentence is significant for two additional reasons: 1. *Men*, set even in the Bible in the italic type, is obviously denoting mankind in general. 2. Jesus is designated as a god, because, according to the relevant myths, only the gods remain always "fully awake" and fully aware.

It is this loss of godhood that was so bitterly lamented by the ancient people, which we have a reflection of in the "stories" such as the Sumerian epic of *Gilgamesh*, or in the Mayan *Popol Vuh*, among others. Yet, these mythological systems not only remember mankind had lost, and regained, this divine capacity at least four or five time in the hoary past, they also promise the current loss was always understood to be the last one. In other words, after about one million years of Guided Evolution, mankind is finally approaching its graduation from this particular "school" of hard knocks, sufficiently "proofed" against any future failures.

That Nostradamus was also somehow aware of the existence of these past cycles is evident in several of his quatrains, of which we shall re-quote here two parts:

> "The world is approaching its final period.
> Saturn will again be returning late ..." 3/92

> "The fatal and eternal order of the cycle
> will return in due order ..." 3/79

In a certain sense though, the statements in these two quatrains contradict each other. In 3/92 the seer speaks of a "final period," that he knew it was, yet, in 3/79 he speaks of an "eternal order of the cycle," since he also somehow knew of their existence in the eons past. Here, though, I would rather put my trust in what the mythological systems have to say on the subject: "Never more. This is the last one."

Now, let us return here, also for the last time, to the subject of the divine state that "petered out" of the human bodies with the demise of the ice age conditions, which Nostradamus describes in words eerily reminiscent of the lamentations found in the *Popol Vuh*.

> "The divine word will be struck by heaven,
> and man won't be able to proceed further.
> To unlock the hidden secret,
> people will have to march on(ward) & ahead." 2/27
>
> "Sublime bodies endlessly visible to the eye.
> For their own reasons they occlude (our) body,
> forehead, major & invisible senses.
> The sacred orations diminish." 4/25

The "divine word" is the sought after Logos, by which power a human deity could know anything, could create anything. It is the essence of human godhood, also known as the Light of life. Here though, we have to read the sentence in the past tense: The Logos was struck by heaven, and from that moment on people were not able to proceed any further as semi-divine beings. "To unlock the hidden secret" of their fate, "people will have to," read "had to," endure the long millennia of history. Such statements, rendered in the future tense, also confirm the very ancient origin of the ideas Nostradamus had the privilege to work with.

The word "sublime" can also be translated as "lofty," or "splendid," and almost certainly refers to the stars, and by extension to the entire Universe. The Universe then, "for (Its) own reasons" had occluded our mind, our senses, which both exist in a more or less dormant state for now. The last line of quatrain 4/25 speaks quite plainly of our severely diminished ability to predict the future, "hinted" at quite often even in *The New Testament*. But this ability is inseparable from presence of the divine substance in our bodies. According to the Indian tradition, in the absence of Shakti, a spiritual substance, even the gods "cannot move." And Shakti is just one of the many names applied to this phenomenon around the world. In India, she is also the flip side of Kali.

As with most of Nostradamus' key predictions, the theme can be corroborated from at least two different quatrains, confirming the correctness of the idea followed. Sometimes such a confirmation though appears in a negative form, as it does in the letter to his son Caesar, where, in the one before the last paragraph he states: "For although they (the human beings) are under a cloud (of mental obscurity), the meanings (of these predictions) will be understood … the case will be cleared up still more." As we doing here.

We can say, with a measured amount of certainty, that our evolution has a definite time limit for its completion, and it is written in capital letters over the evolution of mankind, and over the conditions our solar system found itself in, since about five million years ago. Back then it entered a relatively safe "bubble" of space, virtually free of dense gases and numerous space detritus. About three million years ago the Panama isthmus had closed, which triggered the last period of glaciations, without which our evolution would have been impossible. About 500,000 later appeared the first true human species, the Homo erectus.

The catch is, our solar system is now bound to leave this safe "bubble," to face the real dangers of the Universe. Some astronomers say that might happen in about 1,000 years time, some say in 5,000 years time. Nostradamus, as we shall see, is probably suggesting 7,000 years. In the absence of any definable border in space-time, such differences are almost meaningless. In absolute terms, this event could just as well be taking place tomorrow. But before it does, mankind has to be ready for its role of the defender of Life on this planet, well before the situation arises. Without our protection, the result of hundreds of millions of years of evolution might be wiped out, as nearly happened at least twice before. But rest assured: Mankind will be ready.

We shall close this chapter with a short quote from Nostradamus' letter to his son Caesar, where he again speaks of the transformational processes he described in his prophecies: "Whatever future mutations of mankind will occur …" Nowadays we equate "mutations" with evolutionary cycles. In other words, the seer was somehow aware of the primordial complex process, whose final stage he endeavored to preserve for us, as a warning, but also a road sign to hope, and to our final delivery.

THE NEW ICE AGE

For years we have been hearing about the greenhouse effect. Yet, only recently some climatologists started to realize what has been known long millennia ago, and recorded in myths, or sacred books, like the *Rig Veda*. Namely, that the climate has to warm up first, in order for the moisture to be released into the atmosphere, to facilitate the subsequent glacier build up, and for the glaciers to usher in the next ice age. While the climatologists are still struggling with the real causes of the various ice ages, they have not consulted with the astronomers. Some of those started to realize, also since fairly recently, that the Earth is impacted, on average, once every 3,000 years by an asteroid large enough to influence the climate. And, as we have already noted, what matters for the subsequent climatic effect is not only the size and the composition of such a celestial body, but also where it impacts. That means the latitude, and whether the impact zone is located on land or in a sea, even how deep the sea is. Concerning the impact of the asteroid discussed in this book, Nostradamus makes it quite plain that it will indeed bring about a new period of glaciation.

In several quatrains, he describes "unusual" weather patterns that can only be interpreted as a *sudden* arrival of a new ice age.

> "Mars & Mercury & the Moon join together.
> Towards the south an extreme desiccation ..." 3/3

> "When the downfall of the lunarians approaches,
> they will not be very distant from each other.
> Cold, desiccation, danger around the frontiers,
> even where the oracle had its source." 3/4

In the (first) two lines of quatrain 3/3 we are told that The War, the forces of transformation, and the influence of the Lunar Age will all "join together" in effecting mankind's fate. The "extreme desiccation ... towards the south" is indicating the transfer of moisture towards the polar regions, where it comes down as snow, that will eventually solidify into ice and glaciers. The quatrain 3/4 presents us with a situation near the time of the final defeat of Moslems in Europe." At that time "cold (and) desiccation" will grip even southern France. However, in the letter to his son Caesar, Nostradamus also correctly notes: "Before and after these inundations, in many countries the rains will be so slight ..." as to constitute desiccation. Before the asteroid impact they suffered from the heat; after the impact, and the subsequent climatic shift, from the transfer of moisture towards the poles.

And indeed, we do know that the sub-Saharan region in Africa, as well as the Amazon forest, started to desiccate since at least twenty five years ago. With the ever rising temperatures, the desiccation became more and more pronounced in other parts of the world, including Europe and North America. The new temperature records, the 'slowly' dying Amazon region, and the ever growing number and ferocity of forest fires are a good examples of that.

Perhaps we should reiterate here that the "before and after" desiccation will have two different causes. Before the impact it will be caused by heat alone, which in turn will and does result in vicious floods elsewhere. The desiccation after the impact will be caused exclusively by the cold, but with identical side effect.

To understand why, we have to realize the impact of the asteroid is going to create an instant "asteroid winter," an equivalent of a "nuclear winter," and temperatures will drop dramatically all around the world. Still, the cooling effect will be initially more pronounced in the northern polar region, because it will be more densely shrouded in dust and ejecta from the impact, from the forest fires set ablaze by the passing body of the asteroid. Understandably enough, the global weather patterns will be thrown into chaos.

> "For forty years the rainbow will not appear,
> for forty years it will be seen every day.
> The arid earth will grow more parched,
> and great floods when it will be seen." 1/17

The above quatrain describes quite adequately the chaotic consequence of such a sudden climatic "flip," which will last, we are told, for about forty years, before the climate will settle into a new pattern. During those forty years though, some places will be permanently drenched, as others will suffer from an endless drought. While it might be of little consolation to those afflicted by it, such conditions, of course, did take place in a relatively recent past, and had to be endured even for centuries.

> "The great city of the maritime ocean,
> surrounded by a swamp of crystal.
> During the winter solstice & the spring,
> it will be tried by a dreadful wind." 9/48

The "great city" refers to a capital of a maritime empire. The "swamp of crystal" most likely describes a frozen motley surface, resembling a frozen marsh. By a fairly long stretch of imagination, this city could be London, perhaps some forty years after the impact, as the sea level subsides. But it could also be Paris, or New York, or any other such city, of the former maritime powers, but located along the northern latitude, to be lashed every winter and spring by "a dreadful wind." Essentially though, it hardly matters which of the cities it will be, as more than one will be affected by the same fate. What was important for Nostradamus was to bring to our attention the climatic condition prevalent at such latitudes some fifty years from now.

> "The shining deed of the new old one exalted,
> will be so great in the south and north ..." 10/69

The "new old one" refers, in a mythological fashion, to Artemis, who represented also the last and incomplete link to the preceding "triune goddess" of Thetis / Metis / Themis. Once I translated the names of these ancient "sea goddesses," with the help of the Indo-European dictionary, I realized they all in fact refer to polar glaciers, via the "is" word, or ice, and to the specific sequencing of their "decomposition," or melting, as it occurred during the closing stages of the last Ice Age. Thetis is the "oldest" glacier, and thus the "original" Ice Age glacier, which reconstituted, after a couple thousand years into Metis, the "Middle Ice." When that one substantially diminished, about 7,000 years ago, it reconstituted into Themis, (re: Thames), about 5,200 years ago. Then even Themis started to diminish, to be replaced, at best only symbolically, by Artemis, since perhaps 4,000 years ago. This last stage also represents the smallest volume of glaciation during the last circa 16,000 years.

Yet, Nostradamus is obviously viewing the glaciers as one,

undergoing its metamorphosis, and thus he speaks of "the new old one exalted," or grown again, into its former great self, both at the north and south poles.

> "The earth & air will freeze so much water,
> when they come to venerate on Thursday …" 10/71

The word for Thursday is derived from an old expression of "Thor's day," or the day of Thor, the ancient Norse Jupiter. Since the Jupiter's Age is about to end soon, the only way I can explain the meaning of the two lines above, is in the context of a renewed ancestor worship. As a part of it, the people of the next ice age will come to venerate their ancestors, living through the long, dark, and painful Age of the Jupiter, which started in earnest some 11,700 years ago, and whose unwitting sacrifices will enable them to continue with their evolution, and fulfill their high task. Again, the first line of the above quatrain in fact speaks of large volumes of ice, of glaciers, forming on land.

> "The new empire in desolation.
> It will be changed from the North Pole …" 8/81

The "new empire," referred to in the top line, most likely is the United States of America. The second line, I strongly suspect, has a double meaning: A) Socio-economic conditions will undergo a wholesale transformation, due to the climatic change. B) Due to the same climatic change, advancing from the North Pole, Canada, as a geographical entity, will likely cease to exist. But migrating south, the Canadians will also contribute to these changes, with their stronger sense for law and order, and their left of the centre social inclinations. The millions of refugees from Europe will have a similar contributing influence.

> "Abandoning the fifties and fifty-second degree of latitude,
> they will all render homage to the religions distant from
> the regions of Europe and of the septentrion."
> Letter to Henry II

Since "the fifties … degree of latitude" runs south of England, and through the center of Germany, we can assume that all the places north of that latitude, including most of Russia, will be covered in glaciers, or too close to them to remain habitable, and all such regions will be completely abandoned—or be among the first to be abandoned. As described, the extent of glaciation seems, on the one hand, to exceed the extent during the peak of the previous Ice Age in Western Europe, but it will not be nearly as great in North America.

The reason for that is twofold. As noted below, in quatrain 1/43, Nostradamus had predicted, centuries before the current geologists did, the reversal of magnetic poles. Furthermore, it is now expected by geologists that the north magnetic pole, and thus also the bulk of the polar ice, will be located near the coast of western Siberia, which would result in a much milder ice age conditions in North America.

By the same token, the ice age conditions would also mean the sea level would in time drop by some 150 meters, in comparison to today's level, or perhaps by up to 250 meters, from the level it will reach after the impact. This is a jet-speed oscillation, undreamt of by climatologists, especially not during such a short period of time.

The reference to religions again refers to the abandonment of Christianity in favour of religions "distant" from Europe, or North America, and from the religions of the preceding seven millennia, "the septentrion," in general. In other words, he speaks of a brand new religion, or rather a very ancient one.

> "Before the changes of the Empire arrive,
> a very wonderful event will take place.
> The field moved, the pillar of porphyry
> shifted over the gnarled rock." 1/43

The "changes" implied will commence with the impact of the asteroid. The "field," of course, is the Earth's magnetic field. Porphyry is a volcanic rock, containing fairly large crystals, especially of feldspar. The word "feldspar" in turn is made up of two words: field and pole. Thus, in a "redundant" way Nostradamus is referring to the shift of the magnetic poles. The "gnarled rock," needless to say, is the planet Earth.

NEW CULTURE FOR OLD

In his quatrains Nostradamus does not dwell much on the specifics of a future European culture, because he knew it was fated to end, and its formative role was to be taken up by a new culture.

> "O vast Romanum, your destruction approaches.
> Not of your walls, but of your blood & substance.
> The harsh one in letters will brand a horrid gap.
> Pointed steel reaching all the way up the sleeve." 10/65

Here the word Romanum refers to Europe, as in phrase "the New Holy Roman Empire." What approaches is the destruction of its people, its culture, the "blood & substance" of the European civilization that shaped the modern world. The "harsh one" is Jupiter, or rather the next evolutionary stage. The expression "letters" refers not only to literature and the art of writing, but to the European civilization itself. In fact Nostradamus is saying that, for a time, it will cease to exist.

While it is not meant as a consolation, or to lessen the shattering impact the situation will have on the people affected by the conditions implied, such 'scenarios' did take a place in the past more than once. We know of two such periods, during which the art of writing had ceased to exist, for centuries, within formally civilized societies; namely during the second millennium B.C.E. in the Middle East, and then in Europe, after the fall of the Roman Empire. Also, due to climatic changes, the European population migrated twice during the last 7,000 years alone.

The last line speaks of a sharp pain, cloaked, but reaching the heart.

However, the seer does make one exception, concerning the

future of the European civilization, worth mentioning here.

> "All degrees of Ecclesiastical honour
> will be changed into quirinal Jupiter.
> A martial priest of Quirinus, a man of flames.
> Then a king of France will make him a man of Vulcan." 5/77

In this quatrain Nostradamus is describing an ominous and a rather transitory stage of the French future history. The symbology is appropriately complex, which means we shall have to deal with it in stages. The word "ecclesiastical," to start with, probably has two meanings here: 1) It refers to a priestly class. 2) It also refers to an assembly of citizens. Combined, the expression seems to be designating a new class of "holy warriors," which is more or less confirmed by the third line.

Quirinus used to be a major Roman deity, close in importance to Jupiter and Mars. His name was probably derived from the Latin designation for an assembly of men known as "covirium," and it always had militaristic overtones, especially in the defense aspects of war. In its capacity of a "shield" it can traced back to Egyptian mythology.

Here, however, we also seem to have a direct link to a defense industry, or just a manufacture of arms, of "forging" of weapons in the flame, indicated in the third line.

Vulcan used to be a god of fire, metalworking and craftsmanship, which would only confirm the preceding conclusion. But, as a god of fire, Vulcan also "consumed" bodies of the dead, which is suggested by the last line.

> "Because of the quality of three temporal kings,
> the sacred seat will be put in another place.
> There the substance & the spirit of the body
> will be restored & received as a true seat." 8/99

We shall concern ourselves here only with the first two lines of this splendid quatrain. In the following chapter we shall pick up the theme of the last two lines.

The three "kings" of the top line are the three surviving cultural / language groups of old Europe, namely the French, Germanic, and Slavic. It will be the undefinable qualities that make the leading civilizations the formative forces they are, which will be taken away from the Europeans, and "put in another place." These unique qualities are called in the myths "the golden apples," or "the peaches of immortality." Just like any other fruit, the process of becoming a formative civilization also has its "seasons" of flowering and of bearing "fruits," with one major difference. These "seasons" are each about 3,000 years long. Now, if we think of the "instant" civilizations that rose up in Mesopotamia and Egypt about 6,000 years ago as "the flowering season," we have to admit those cultures have passed into insignificance about 3,000 years ago, just as the European culture, embodied back then in the Greeks and the Etruscans, took up the role of a formative civilization. In spite many reservations about its overall success, this civilization did deliver the "fruits" one would expect from a high civilization. This 'season' though is now over as well and the time to begin anew is almost upon us, albeit on an entirely different level.

The "other place," where the sacred seat is being transferred to is, of course, North America. More specifically to the United States, to which Nostradamus devotes quite a few quatrains.

> "Libra is going to rule the Hesperides,
> the sky & earth under its control ..." 4/50

If you remember, Hercules brought the Golden Apples from the Garden of Hesperides, located somewhere in north-western Africa, where a splendid civilization blossomed, for about 3,000 years, from circa 8,000 to 5,000 years ago. The places he would have brought them to would have been Mesopotamia and Egypt, which would have become the next such Garden. The still current Garden of the Hesperides is Europe, although the process of transference is now undoubtedly well under way to the North American continent, facilitated by the same "Hercules," also known as the Saviour of Pure and Unmixed Spirit. Incidentally, his name means "Glory of Hera," and Hera, also known as the "Lady," or the "Holy One," and the Mother of gods, in turn is the Mother Earth herself.

The astrological sign of Libra is always represented by the scales, which most likely is the only reason why Nostradamus chose that image. The scales of Justice in turn are virtually a synonym for Liberty, represented by the colossal statue in New York harbour.

In other words, Justice and Liberty will continue their reign in the United States, the new Hesperia, for a long time to come, since this continent was fated to experience both the flowering and the fruiting seasons, as we shall see in the next chapter. In the balance of this one, I would like to relate the earliest history of the United States, as seen through a number of Nostradamus' quatrains.

"European newcomers will build a place without defenses,
occupying a place inhabitable till then:
Meadows, houses, fields, towns taken with joy.
Famine, plague, war, extensive arable land." 2/19

At the time Nostradamus was writing the quatrains, America was barely known in Europe, and the European population there was very scarce. At the same time, while the first settlements in North America were protected by palisades, a form of fortification Nostradamus terms "defenses," in Europe of the times every town, even villages and monasteries and some individual churches were fortified. However, the seer is talking about communities without fortifications, which did not become the norm even in North America until the mass migration had started. The second line plainly states that the place was in fact inhabitable, but barely populated. The third line describes, in a very abbreviated fashion, the process of colonization. The last line, by and large, refers to the fate suffered by the Amerindians, and to the abundance of available arable land on the 'new' continent.

"The well off sister of the island of Britain
will be born fifteen years before her brother.
Because her promise will be verified,
she will succeed to rule the balance." 4/96

The "well off sister" is, of course, the United States, whose "birthday" is the year 1774, when the Declaration of Rights was drawn up during the First Continental Congress in Philadelphia. The "brother" of this "well off sister" is the French revolution, modeled on the American ideals of freedom and equality, which started in 1789, exactly fifteen years after the birth of the United States. The statement "well off sister" alone foretold the future prosperity of the United States, and of its population, in comparison to her imperial "sister."

Because the historical, or rather the evolutionary promise, rooted in freedom and self-organization, expressed in form of various volunteer organizations, will hold out to be true in the long run, America "will succeed to rule the balance." The balance represented by the scales of Justice, the Libra of quatrain 4/50, but applied to all the Life on this planet. However, as we already know, and as we can glean from Nostradamus' quatrains, the road to such a lofty goal will be neither straight, nor too easy.

"The free city of liberty becomes a servant,
a refuge for profligates & dreamers.
The rule changes and is not so violent to them.
The hundred will grow into more than a thousand." 4/16

The "free city" is any city in the United States. The word "profligate" can be defined as being amoral, recklessly wasteful, which perfectly describes modern capitalism, originating and flourishing currently in the United States. The "rule," or the law, was predicted to come to tolerate, virtually encourage such behaviour, as we know it did, and does. The last line refers either to the quickly growing population in general, or equally, to the fast increase in the number of the "profligates & dreamers." For the better and for the worse, it was these characters that have, to a very noticeable extent, helped to make America what it is today.

"Garden of the world near the New City
(transformed) into the road of the hollow mountains.
It will be seized & plunged into the tank,
forced to drink water poisoned with sulfur." 10/49

The expression "garden of the world" evokes a picture of pristine, almost paradisiacal state of nature. In a fairly plain language, the second line tells us that this "garden" will be transformed "into the road of the hollow mountains," that is into a street between rows of skyscrapers. Considering that the ziggurats and the pyramids were the representation of a heavenly mountain, the idea of a "hollow mountain" is a fairly apt description for such gigantic buildings, most of which are office buildings, housing large corporations.

Since it is rather difficult to imagine such a transformed garden could be "plunged into a tank," we have to assume Nostradamus was resorting to the most appropriate substitute imagery available to him at the time. The key word to unraveling the image is the word "sulfur." Even with my limited knowledge of chemistry, I know that no gas can permanently bind with water to act as poison, but is bound to bubble through it. To understand what Nostradamus was attempting to describe, we have to imagine a heavily polluted downtown of a contemporary American city, especially during an atmospheric inversion, on a hot summer day, to comprehend that the haze caused by the combination of such effects, and actually heavily saturated with sulfur, could appear almost as thick as water to someone who has never seen anything of that sort. Needless to add, lots of people nowadays are "forced to drink," that is to breathe the polluted air.

> "When Europe will be covered by the Sun,
> under the splendor will be a hidden form.
> Mercury will expose the aura of fire,
> yet (Europe) insulted by a rumour of war." 4/28

This quatrain is not exactly very clear, but the first line seems to be referring to the "Americanization" of the European culture, after the World War II. The "hidden form" most likely represents the increasing frictions and resentments between the two cultures, growing lately ever more apart. The last two lines probably refer to the current geo-political situation, with Mercury again representing the transformation process, fraught with acute dangers, which the Europeans, sick of wars, willfully keep on ignoring.

> "The law of the Sun contending with Europe,
> appropriating the spirit of prophecy.
> Neither the one nor the other will be understood.
> The Sun will retain the law of the great Messiah." 5/53

This quatrain essentially repeats the message of the preceding one. The Sun, that is the U.S., because of its current aggressive policies in confronting the Moslem revivalists / terrorists, will be seen, in hind sight, to have possessed almost a prophetic gift, in view of the future invasion of Europe. However, the two partners do not understand each other for two reasons: 1. The White House administration is seen in Europe to act, in general, out of crass economic interests. 2. We are still unable to comprehend that nation-states too, as individuals, can act on an unconscious level, thus fulfilling their fated roles.

By "retain(ing) the law," America, being herself "the great Messiah" of the future, will uphold its relevant obligations, and when the time will be ready, "deliver" the surviving Europeans from the Moslem oppression. In fact America will most likely assume the role of the greatest Messiah of them all, Hercules, whose task was to save "his people," that is all the people of this planet, from extinction, by providing them with the structure and tools for their (non-existent) cultures, and by assisting in their ecological tasks. In order to do that, America will be able to retain its material and organizational capacity.

"Under the faint pretext of removing servitude,
the city & the people themselves usurp power.
Worse off, because of a trickery of a young whore,
traitor to the field, pursuing the wrong promise." 5/5

This quatrain represents a definition of a populist democracy in a nutshell. Where Ortega y Gasset needed an entire book, his famous "*The Revolt of the Masses*," to describe the degrading effect of such a system on all social standards, Nostradamus makes do with four short lines of text.

We have to keep in mind that, at least philosophically, the populist oriented democracies are the result of bourgeois revolutions, whose goal was to further the economic and social interests of their class. Thus the line "faint pretext of removing servitude," because the masses ended up serving the new masters. Since such a 'democracy' can survive only with a wide popular support, it has to, at least nominally, cater to the needs and wants of the broad masses. To accomplish that, cultural and intellectual standards of the entire society were gradually reduced to their level of understanding. By the time such an 'adjustment' is completed, the leading intellectual element is all but gone, or serves the plutocrats, one way or the other, it can be said that "the people themselves usurp power," as any signs of mental independence and intellectual vigor are gone. And since most people live in cities, where all the corporations are also headquartered, the cities in fact "usurp power," at the expense of nature.

The third line is suggesting that the people will end up worse off than they were, "because of a trickery of a young whore." This "young whore," I suspect, are the sciences that, in general, sold out to the plutocrats. And not just the material sciences, but all sciences subject to the Darwinian dogma, such as the ill conceived 'theory' of evolution. By the same token, it is also the new form of impersonal rapacious would-be-capitalism, whose proponents care for nothing else but money, in which every aspect of the society is therefore focused on money. As a result, the masses are worse off not only morally and spiritually, but also financially, because in this day and age they have to work a lot harder for what they earn, than people did some 100 years ago. Jointly, the plutocrats, the scientists, and the masses, are also "traitor(s) to the field," with the "field" representing Nature. They betrayed Nature by the wholesale plunder of her resources, and in the process continue to destroy her.

The populist democracy was to have guaranteed a well being for the masses in perpetuity. Yet, as some social thinkers are already saying, people could soon end up being worse off than they ever were. Being dependent solely and totally on their city jobs, many of them, and eventually most of them, would become completely disenfranchised and helpless if they were to lose, first jobs, then social assistance, of any kind, especially after the expected collapse of the economy. Furthermore, it is "the wrong premise," because, within decades, we are bound to run out of all the non-renewable resources, without which this materialistic civilization cannot go on, starting with some of the rare earth elements, some of which will be gone within mere years.

"For the pleasure of decreed sensuality,
poison will be mixed with the law.
Venus will be virtuous at the court,
all the solar glory will be obscured." 5/72

To decree sensuality presupposes either perverted lawgivers, or ignorant of the consequences of their good intentions. Such, unfortunately, was the case with one item in the American Bill of Rights, "the law," specifically the part that speaks of "the pursuit of happiness," because most people started to equate "happiness" with material well being and its pursuit. But when this becomes translated into excessive accumulation of ever bigger homes, cars, TVs, fridges, into overindulgence in food, booze, drugs, sex, and other bodily pleasures, we are talking of a cult of sensuality, of "decreed sensuality."

Venus, in this case, via Venice, represents the big business. Its interests, the "poison," as Nostradamus predicts, will exert an unprecedented influence "at the court." Linguistically, the word "court" has two relevant meanings here: 1) A court of law. 2) The "royal court," which has to be read as the seat of power in the United States, namely the Senate and the House of Representatives, as well as the White House. We can correctly assume the quatrain alludes to all of them. Because of this influence though, "all solar glory" of the United States "will be obscured." In other words, the world will see only the negative aspects of the American culture, and remain unaware of the tendency of the population for self-reliance, self-organization, co-operation, for helping the follow human beings, represented by the plethora of volunteer, co-op organizations, that each count about half of the population among its members. Yet, it is exactly these qualities that are very much in compliance with the Great Universal Law that will in time turn North America into the formative civilization of the Solar Age.

We should also add here that the "poison" of the above quatrain can be equated to the "trickery" of quatrain 5/5, even to the chemical poison of quatrain 10/49.

> "The rule & law raised under Venus —
> Saturn shines upon Jupiter's empire.
> Law & rule raised by the Sun
> will endure the worst for the Saturnians." 5/24

Here, again, we can see how Nostradamus switches symbols, and / or overlaps them. Here Venus should stand for Europe, the "rule & law" of the Western culture. However, since the Western culture also has to include the United States, the implication points to the removal of "the rule & law raised under Venus," that is under the plutocratic auspices of the American, or "Jupiter's empire," through the influence of the new Saturnian era. "Law & rule raised by the Sun" refers, in fact, to the transformative qualities of freedom and cooperation, that originated in North America, and which "will endure the worst" of the turbulent period, and prevail, for the sake of the future generations, that is of "the Saturnians," the people of the Saturn's Age.

> "One day adversity will cease between the two great masters,
> their great power seen to increase.
> The new land will be at the peak of its power,
> to the bloody one the number is reported." 2/89

This quatrain portrays the present situation, pertaining to the relationship between the United States and Russia, and the current position of dominance occupied by the United States, "the new land." The "bloody one" is Jupiter, or Artemis, during the coming decades of the 21st century. The "reported number" is the seventh millennium, according to the biblical count. This quatrain is important 'only' so far as it correctly predicts the geo-political situation in the world at the turn of the 20th and 21st centuries. But it also tells us that soon after the U.S. power peaks, the wholesale transformation will start. But, before it starts, the U.S. will also experience the humiliation of a total economic collapse and bankruptcy.

"The imitations of gold & silver inflated,
and after the rape thrown into a burning lake.
Upon discovery will fall into a troubled silence.
All stocks and bonds will be worthless." 8/28

"The imitations of gold & silver," one can be reasonably sure, is the grossly over-valued U.S. dollar, pumped up by the annual investments of hundreds of billions of dollars from abroad. The expression "after the rape," lets you pick any country invaded for its oil or gas, or an action connected somehow to these, suggested by the idea of the "burning lake," and the currency will dramatically plunge in value, due also in part to the staggering $17 trillion in federal debt. The collapse will wreak havoc two ways: 1. Massive sell off of American dollars, of government and corporate bonds and stocks, which will make "all stocks and bonds worthless." 2. The American and the global economies will collapse. This will, of course, represent very bad news not only for the investors and the corporation, but for the bulk of the American population, all stunned "into a troubled silence," because so many will lose their jobs. But the impoverishment of the middle class, and of many in the upper class as well, along with the exposure of the structural weakness and criminal manipulation of the system, will also make the subsequent social transformation that much easier. The outcome of that, at least on the North American continent, in spite the temporary "inconveniences," will make it all worthwhile. Yet, no matter how the future economic events will shape up, the above quatrain will be fulfilled, more or less to the letter.

Also, since the material sciences and technology represent an important part of the old order, we have to reflect here on their origin and their ultimate fate as well.

To start with, we know that Nostradamus alluded in over twenty quatrains to planes, submarines, space satellites, amphibious vehicles, skyscrapers, pollution, to computers, nuclear weapons and the consequences of their use, even to the landing on the Moon.

In this respect, science and technology have to be seen as a part of the larger picture of the predicted reality, and as such have to be viewed as a form of a "natural force" permeating our Guided Evolution, rather than something explicitly "man-made." As we have already noted, in order to fulfill its destiny, mankind will need such tools—albeit to serve a very different goal than they do today.

Incongruously enough, the Benedictine theologian / philosopher

Erigena saw the desired goal way back in the 9th century. While he referred to technology as "mechanical arts," he, and his successors, had invested these with spiritual significance. The reasoning behind such perception was fairly straightforward: "The destiny of man as *imago dei* and his vocation as the follow worker of God … (was) to co-operate with God in the establishment of His Kingdom," as summarized for us historian Ernst Benz.

That, indeed, was a truly genuine, revolutionary thinking, because, while technology was in a sporadic use for millennia, it was never thought of as being in the service of God's creation.

Wind and water powered mills of all sorts were known for ages. The Roman emperor Nero used a steam engine in his boat. Aluminum was made in Rome and in China. Unbreakable glass was also invented in Rome. Electrolysis was used at least 3,000 years ago in Mesopotamia, and glass lenses were in fairly wide use, for a variety of purposes, throughout the classical world. Even geared computing devices for navigation were in existence more than 2,000 years ago. As Erigena correctly argued, such abilities were indeed always a part of mankind's original endowment.

It was in the 12th century France that Cistercian monks have reintroduced, on a "massive scale," an assortment of simple technologies to Western Europe, at their great mother abbey in Clairvaux. This step was described as a veritable medieval industrial revolution.

Then, about 500 years later, Sir Francis Bacon proposed the idea of systematic scientific research, while at the same time pleading with the scientists not to jump to any premature conclusions about their discoveries. Virtually to a man, and the odd woman, they have been jumping to premature conclusions ever since, distorting in the process our concept and perception of reality. In a 'side effect', the concepts proposed by both Erigena and Francis Bacon were abandoned. Yet, even this turn of events was likely unavoidable, as we were meant to learn our painful lesson from such mistakes.

In general, we could say that, having predicted certain technological achievements centuries ago, Nostradamus also predicted the sciences that brought the technology into existence. In a sense then, the modern sciences have existed, in a "negative" state, since centuries ago, waiting to be "developed" by the proper "chemicals," that is by appropriate socio-historical circumstances. And these, in turn, were also prepared by the Supreme Being.

Sometimes the needed ideas appeared prematurely, such as the design for a staged rocket in 17th century, or the friar Mendel's genetic concepts in 18th century, and simply had to wait their turn. But when the time was "right," identical inventions often came in twos, even threes.

There is only one way to explain such multiple urges: our subconscious. In fact, many of the key ideas of modern sciences were literally "dreamt up," as scientific laws, or inventions, arrived, to those who were well prepared to receive them, in their sleep, or while they slumbered, or when out for a relaxing walk.

But these would be only the most blatant, and in a sense 'exaggerated' examples. But then, "many studies ... confirm that human beings can and do perceive complex, even symbolic information in the absence of any conscious awareness and can and do respond to the information perceived in a highly appropriate customary sensible way," states Barbara B. Brown in her book "*Supermind*."

When deciding where the perceived information came from, Dr. Brown, who pioneered the biofeedback technique, answers with a question: "Is there ... the possibility that still another 'law' of evolution exists, a peculiar force of energy ... that is the unifying principle of nature hovering over evolution, directing its destiny?"

David Bohm, the brightest star of the quantum mechanics, answers this question in a more affirmative way: "Life is no longer seen as the result of somewhat fortuitous factors ... rather it is seen to be enfolded universally, deep within the generative order." To this he adds: "Orders of the kind discussed ... maybe called a kind of 'proto intelligence'. This does not refer to a conscious awareness but to the active generation of a new order." At the same time he said: "... the generative order enfolds orders that go beyond those that can be contained even in the quantum domain, orders that have been so far 'hidden' to science."

To sum up the above, we can say that both, our science and our technology are the result of a subconscious processes, during which the human mind acts with all its will and logic upon the impulses received in a subliminal way from the Supreme Being, perhaps through the quantum magnetic fields, as if these impulses have truly originated in our conscious minds. Yet, after mankind will fully emerge from the Moon Age, people will be able to receive such instructions consciously. By then, of course, the sciences will be in the service of creation, instead of acting against it.

SPIRIT REBORN

When Jesus in effect promised that people will be "like angels, like gods," in the coming Kingdom of God, he again merely echoed the promise made by the ancient myths that foretold the return of the Golden Age, which in turn can be equated to the Kingdom of God.

Some of the myths, instead of the Golden Age, refer to such periods as the Sun Age. Needless to say, the mythological references to "two suns" have seriously confused the few historians, including E.A. Wallis Budge, who have bothered to pay attention to these 'odd' signals in Egyptian scripts. Nostradamus writes about such a "second sun" in quatrain 4/29:

> "The hidden Sun transformed by Mercury
> will be placed only second in the heavens ..."

Of course, there were never two sun stars shining in the Earth's sky, nor there will ever be in the future. The "second sun" represents the symbol for spiritual and creative power, the inner light humans shone with before the Age of the Moon, and will shine again, once it is gone, during the appropriately named Age of the Sun, which is going to dispel, abolish, even a hint of mental darkness.

In "practical" terms, it means the mental capacity of ordinary humans, when compared to today's capacity, will be much, much greater. This will arise from an increase of the human cranium by perhaps circa 25 percent, and by circa 50 percent increase in the number of neuron connections, starting with the generation born twenty years after the asteroid impact, as spelled out below. The incredible increase in the number of interconnected neurons will not only tremendously improve our capacity for memory and thinking, but will also improve our perception, and our ability to communicate with our very bodies, and thus enable us to maintain healthy bodies. "No one who dwells there will say 'I am sick' …" (Isaiah 33-24) Here the word "there" refers to the so called Kingdom of God.

It goes without saying, such a brain will radically improve evolutionary advantage over the present "model," especially thanks to its ability to foresee, and hopefully to resolve virtually all of the problems looming ahead. In this respect, people are meant to resemble the ancient god Prometheus, whose very name means Foresight. What the myth about his return in fact tells us is that it was the human foresight that was "chained," some 12,000 years ago, and is about to return with the new ice age.

> "When twenty years of the Moon's reign have passed,
> for seven thousand years the other will rule.
> When the Sun will tackle the days allowed to it,
> then accomplished my threats & my prophecies." 1/48

This quatrain is quite plainly telling us that the Sun Age will commence twenty years after the asteroid impact. This prophecy is "echoed" by the Mayan prediction, found in their sacred book *Chilam Balam*. Selecting only the relevant highlights from it, we can piece together this text:

"On the day 13 Ahau the katun will end (and) a new day shall dawn in the north … the day of our regeneration comes … let us exalt his sign on high … the First Tree of the World restored, it is displayed to the world. This is the sign of Hunab-Ku (the Supreme Being) on high … it came from heaven … You shall be converted to the world of Hunab-Ku … They will correct their ways who receive him in their hearts in another katun …"

As you can see, many identical themes appear here that we have found in Nostradamus prophecies: The First Tree displayed to the world is the impact site of the asteroid, "in the north," almost a mirror image of Nostradamus' "rose of the world." The "world of Hunab-Ku" is the "Kingdom of God," aka the new Sun Age. The date 13 Ahau corresponds to December 21st, 2012, and a "katun" is a twenty year long period of time.

In spite the fact that Nostradamus and the Mayans are in full agreement, regarding the beginning of the Sun Age, if not about the date, the mental / spiritual transformation will not, regrettably, be effecting the people already born within the period designated as the Moon Age, but only the children that will start to be born during the new ice age, some twenty years after the impact, whenever that may be.

As far as our understanding of the unraveling of future events on the North American continent is concerned, the fact that the Sun "will take up the reign for 7,000 years" is very important. Again, most likely, for two reasons: 1) The Sun stands here for North America, which will become the formative civilization, providing cultural standards for the entire world for the next 7,000 years. 2) It also says that the "flowering" and "fruiting" seasons, of 3,000 years each, will no longer apply. Nor will the other time cycles.

> "Libra will reign in the Hesperides,
> holding the rule over the skies & the earth." 4/50

As we already know, the name Hesperides is bestowed upon any formative civilization and, without a question, North America is the future Hesperia. "Libra," representing the scales of justice, as symbolized by the statue of Liberty in New York, will reign on in that part of the world. And since North America will also be "holding the rule over the skies & the earth" of the entire world, presumably justice and liberty will equally reign all over the world, as will the concept of responsibilities towards the planet, once the Sun Age is fully established.

The second line of quatrain 1/48 also "hints" at the possibility that the coming Sun Age might either be suspended, or transformed, some 7,000 later, or that the American cultural dominance will pass.

As I explain elsewhere, our solar system is bound to enter the nasty regions of the universe, full of space dust and detritus. To compensate for these obstacles, our Sun will increase its output, which also means it will get warmer on this planet, as scientists now realize. However, mankind will have those 7,000 years to prepare for this change, and be able to deal with it—even if their mental / spiritual capacity might revert closer to the current levels. For example, a suitable space "umbrella" could compensate for an excessive increase in the Sun's output, and help to maintain the "ice age" conditions, if required. By the same token, at this stage we simply cannot foresee what solutions to the problem mankind will be able to conceive of, especially if inspired by the negative option.

The last line of quatrain 1/48 clearly tells us that Nostradamus' prophecies will all be accomplished at that stage, which still points towards the second half of the 21st century.

Understandably, the mental / spiritual transformation, as well as the socio-economic change on the North American continent will be gradual, starting with conscious acceptance of the Supreme Being, that we can refer to as the quantum, or Q-God, and also the acceptance of the role assigned to mankind by this entity.

> "Through the powers of three temporal kings
> the sacred seat will be put in another place,
> where the substance & the spirit of the body
> will be restored & received as the true seat." 8/99

The temporal "kings" will be the three surviving European 'races', the French, the Germanic, and the Slavic. But it will be rather the loss of their powers that will put "the sacred seat," the Hesperian seat, in "another place," which we have already concluded is North America. The restoration of "the substance & the spirit of the body" will most likely commence there before all the other places, starting perhaps those twenty years after the impact, but likely sooner. The sentence "received as a true seat" seems to suggest two meanings: 1) The Hesperian seat will finally secure a true lasting home. 2) The newly restored incorruptible human body will, once again, become the true seat for the Supreme Being to reside in as well.

Since the notion of "incorruptible body" needs an explanation, we should point out that the newly expanded mind, as a host of hints in ancient myths, and certain findings in biofeedback, microbiology and quantum mechanics suggest, should be able to communicate directly with "its" body, and to have the knowledge and ability to completely repair any malfunctioning part of it, with the likely exception of invading viruses, thus offering people prospects of extreme longevity. The other option that will become available to some of these semi-divine beings, will be the opportunity to receive communication directly from the Supreme Being, to know what this Entity knows about the past and the future —and thus be able to "prophecy," as is promised also in the Bible. Furthermore, through the same "communication channel" the humans will be able to contact similarly evolved sentient beings throughout the entire Universe—instantly—and to learn about their home worlds, without the need to travel there.

Such a state, of course, will not be arrived at overnight, but be preceded by series of economic, social and religious upheavals.

> "When those of the cross find their senses troubled,
> in place of sacred things a horned bull.
> The pig will fully replace the virgin,
> the king will no longer maintain the order." 8/90

In this context, "those of the cross" is a metaphor for all of those who literally believe in what the cross represents—the orthodox Christians. The image of the bull is little more difficult to explain, since it contains more than one meaning. Essentially, the bull represents the might human beings can rise to, and the periodic, albeit unwilling sacrifice of it. For example, in the ancient Book of Enoch, the Messiah is represented as a white bull. By the same token, the supreme god of the Semitic people in the Middle East, El, who was identified as the Sun, was often portrayed as a bull. Zeus, kidnapping Europa, was masquerading as a bull a well. Then there was the famous Mithraic "cult," focused on a bull's sacrifice. The ancient Egyptians also practiced a "cult" of a bull, portraying Ra, their Sun-god, as one. And the Athenian legends of the Moirae, or Fates, compared all men to sacrificial bulls. From such 'hints' though we can also conclude that people of those periods also saw themselves and their ancestors as the sacred sacrifice on the altar of evolution.

In mythological stories the Mother Earth devouring her children is represented by a pig. It is this 'pig' that will replace the Virgin Mary in the minds of most people. Obviously, the two middle lines of the above quatrain have a lot in common. In fact genocide, in this context, becomes a sacrificial slaughter of a large number of human beings. Yet the omens presented there are not all bad, because the quatrain also suggests that people will start perceiving not just the everyday reality, but also their religion(s) with different eyes, adjusting their minds more to the demands placed on them by the Supreme Being.

The last line probably contains two different meanings, both of them correct: 1. In the above context, the would be "divine king," that is Jesus and his Church, "will no longer be able to maintain the order," that is the religious order, i.e. Christianity itself. 2. It also applies to the secular "king," that is the government of the time, which "will no longer be able to maintain the order" either. The result will be anarchy. Some places temporary, some places rather of long duration.

> "Monk's and nun's child exposed to death,
> to die by a she bear & carried off by a boar ..." 9/10

Again, the monk's and nun's "child" is nothing else but the Church, "conceived" by the clergy. It will be exposed to the elements of the times. The "she bear," as already explained, is Artemis, the goddess of the Bear Cult and the punitive aspect of "Mother Earth." The "boar," or wild pig, is "Mother Earth," in her devouring aspect. However, since monks and nuns exist in most religions, the same fate can be expected for all of them, not just the Christian one.

> "Temples consecrated in the original Roman fashion
> will reject the broken foundations,
> taking up their original & human laws,
> chasing out almost all the cults of the saints." 2/8

The original Roman temples were dedicated to Artemis, this time as the "she-wolf" who suckled, the story claims, Romulus and Remus, the two fabled founders of Rome. This renewed religion of Artemis will then "reject the broken foundations" of the existent churches, and take up its "original & human laws." These laws, in turn, are inseparable from the concepts of Guided Evolution and of human destiny, to which the current human laws will have to adapt to, along with the conduct of the entire society, including the current churches. Consequently, "almost all the cults of the saints" will be chased out.

> "A man will be charged with destruction
> of temples & sects altered by fantasy.
> He will harm the stones rather than the living,
> filling the ears with ornate speeches." 1/96

This quatrain is more or less self-explanatory. Still, one man obviously would not be adequate to such a task, and the destruction will most likely be accomplished by those ornate, or rather learned speeches, explaining the real facts of life on this planet to the congregations. The physical churches will either topple during the planet-quake, or they will be temporarily used for other purposes, such as sheltering the great masses of refugees. Yet some, no doubt, will suffer from the wrath of the enraged mob, and be vandalized, burned, or otherwise destroyed.

The expression “fantasy” unmistakably refers to the Bible. The Old Testament is really nothing else but a collection of historicized mythological fragments, woven into fantastic stories. That is stories lacking not only in reality, but also lacking in truths, spun for the sole benefit of the Jewish temple in Jerusalem. The roots of the New Testament also sprung from the same ground.

Of course, changes in the spiritual / religious sphere will go hand in hand with the changes in the society at large, as is suggested in the following quatrain.

> “There will be peace, union & change.
> Estates and offices from low to high & from high to low.
> Preparation for the journey torments the main fruit.
> War to cease, civil process, debates.” 9/66

This quatrain seems to be tailor made for North America. Obviously, it implies a previous presence of an armed conflict, or most likely of a civil war, arising from the state of anarchy, after the asteroid’s impact. Yet, this transitory stage will be fairly brief, and it will be followed by peace, and a renewal of the union, albeit on a new foundation. Thus the “change.” As a result of it, the former ruling classes, the plutocrats and their rich servants of all kinds, i.e. “the main fruit,” of the current civilization, will be removed from their positions of power and influence. And, of course, the very prospect of such a change is going to “torment” these characters, being relegated from a willful near godhood to ordinary folks. But obviously unable to change the outcome of the situation, they will be forced to toss the towel in. Then this war will cease, the civil process will start, and so will the debates about the future form of the society, forced to do away with the power principle. It would also seem that the position of the last line and of the first line should be reversed, in order to perceive the proper sequence of events.

> “He will come to expose the false topography,
> the urns of the hidden monuments revealed.
> Sect of holy philosophy will thrive,
> black for white & the new for the old.” 7/14

The above quatrain only confirms what was said before, by reintroducing the mysterious “he.” The “topography” of the society, its orientation points, are its philosophy, its collection of values, which, in our case, are practically all misplaced, or false. They will be replaced by the true values, long "buried" in deep underground "tombs" of our subconscious, and in myths. The newly established "sect of holy philosophy" will eventually rectify all the current and future problems, transform and rejuvenate the society.

> "Before long, everything will be organized.
> We await a very sinister century.
> The state of the masked & solitary ones greatly changed.
> Few will find who wish to retain their rank." 2/10

In this quatrain the second line should be the first one, to fit the context, because the second line refers, essentially, to the 20th century. "… for the whole of Europe and Russia, this (20th) century became a time out of hell," during which some 70 million people were killed, writes George Steiner in his *Grammars of Creation*. Then he also concedes our very humaneness has lapsed during that "very sinister century." And not just in Europe. Perhaps even more so in the United States, for entirely different reasons, that have everything to do with the most rapacious and destructive form of modern exploitative capitalism.

However, in quatrain 1/51 Nostradamus explains further that this "very sinister century" will last noticeably longer than 100 years: "Then the bad times will return after a long century." The 20th century that killed enough people, and delivered enough technological inventions to fill, from the seer's perspective, many centuries, could as well be described a "long century." The "bad times" of wars and suffering will return after the impact of the asteroid. Interestingly enough, if one was to count the "very sinister (long) century" from 1914 to 2014, the quatrain 1/51 de facto suggests the asteroid impact will take place after 2014, as I realized only during the last re-write of this book.

The rest of the quatrain 2/10 then complements the quatrain 10/66. It in fact confirms that the North American civil war will be fairly short, and soon after it is over, "everything will be organized" the way it will need to be organized.

The "masked & solitary ones" are not only the plutocrats, hiding their power behind the smokescreen of populist democracy, but also their servant scientists, hiding their often reckless and extremely dangerous work behind the multiple walls of anonymity, jargon, blinkered specialization and a convoluted dogma. More or less the same can be said about most politicians and the unelected and inaccessible hierarchy of bureaucrats.

On the other hand, as Nostradamus predicts, once things "will be organized," very few of these formally "masked & solitary ones" will "wish to retain their rank." The reason for that will be the overwhelming evidence that any resistance to this makeover would be utterly futile. And a key part of this evidence will be the fulfillment of these predictions, the confirmation of the Supreme Being's continued involvement in our affairs.

> "The religion named after the seas will prevail
> against the sect of the son Adaluncatif.
> The obstinate, deplored sect afraid
> of the two, wounded by Aleph & Aleph." 10/96

In this quatrain only the first line, unfortunately, is easy to interpret. Yet, fortunately, it is ultimately also the only one here that really matters. The "sea," in most ancient languages, was "mare," or "mari." The seas are where all life originated, and the seas will also be the "home" to large portions of the future polar glaciers. The seas also represent the key component of the hydraulic cycle that maintains life on this planet, and provide a major portion of the oxygen life needs, while removing much of the carbon dioxide life forms exhale. Without the seas and their "protection," life, as we know it, could not exist on this planet. In this respect it is also possible that certain aspects of the Marian cult will survive in this new religion, because, for example, the sky-blue cloak of Saint Mary is known as "the cloak of protection." On the other hand, people will also remember the awesome destructive power the sea can unleash, and respect it, "revere it," as one of the two aspects of a dual "goddess."

The remaining three lines represent enough challenge to admit to a healthy dose of speculation on my part. The name Adaluncatiff is obviously a made up one, possibly consisting of: Adam, Lunar, and Catiff. The first two names seem to fit the picture. The third one is an open ended puzzle. It could refer to the Babylonian serpent goddess Kadi, to Cato the elder, a Roman senator known as "the censor," and a couple of other examples with nasty implications. If I had to commit myself, I would declare this sect to be either the plutocrats or, more likely, Christianity as represented by Jesus. The "two," most likely, are the two polar glaciers, previously "wounded," i.e. diminished "by Aleph & Aleph," which can be no other than the Supreme Being, the bottomless well of all new beginnings, in contrast to Yahweh, who was designated as Alpha & Omega, the Beginning & the End, which could also signify only a temporal and temporary god, where Alpha & Alpha represents an Eternal Beginning, a process of renewal. Of course the "deplored sect" would fear the growth of the polar glaciers, because the more they would grow, the more their prospects would diminish, as more and more people's eyes and minds would continue to gradually open.

While this might not be the most steadfast interpretation, its details fit the overall pattern presented by Nostradamus.

What follows now is a string of quatrains, or parts of quatrains, focused on the renewal of our mental / spiritual potential, that has been obscured for long centuries or, one should say, millennia.

> "The lost thing is discovered, hidden for long centuries …
> … This is when the Moon completes her cycle …" 1/25
>
> "The tree which had been dead and withered a long time
> will flourish again in one night …" 3/91
>
> "The bones of the feet & the hands ensnared,
> because of the noise the house is uninhabited for a long time.
> Digging for dreams, they will be unearthed,
> the house healthy & inhabited without noise." 7/41
>
> "More than eleven times the Moon does not want the Sun,
> both raised & lessened to a degree …" 4/30

The "lost thing" of quatrain 1/25 is the human mental / spiritual potential to be "discovered" or rather rediscovered, "when the Moon completes her cycle," which we know will be twenty years after the impact of the asteroid. The "tree" of quatrain 3/91 is the proverbial Tree of Life. While the "one night" refers to the impact that will change everything, we know that the real flourishing will have to wait a few decades.

The first line of quatrain 7/41 is attempting to describe the mental stagnation, or paralysis, mankind had to endure during the long night of its mental / spiritual sleep. The "noise," also mentioned in Mesopotamian myths, alludes to the noise of our wars, and of our needless commercial activities, the cries of hapless masses in an agony of seemingly endless suffering, whose causes they fail to comprehend. This noise in fact had filled the space reserved for the Supreme Being, or if you wish, the voice of Nature.

The "uninhabited house" is the empty space within us, vacated by the Supreme Being.

We have already encountered the quatrain 4/30 in the previous chapter. It is here to refresh our memory, and to confirm that during the twelfth millennium of the long night of our mental sleep, the Moon (Age) will finally "accept," i.e. be replaced by, the Sun (Age), after more than eleven millennia of "refusals." The second line also informs us that, in the past, partial transpositions, or "false dawns" of the Sun Age did occasionally take place; for example during the peak of the Little Ice Age. This was also the period during which Nostradamus composed his quatrains.

> "The body without a soul no longer being sacrificed.
> The day of death turned into rebirth.
> The divine spirit will make the soul rejoice,
> seeing the Word in its eternity." 2/13

As the above quatrain spells out quite clearly, at this stage, each of us is deemed to be a being without a soul. The soul, in turn, can be deemed the ability of our minds to become consciously aware of the Supreme Being, and to share of Its knowledge. This is just a different way of saying the Supreme Being will "reside in our bodies."

"The day of death," the day of the asteroid's impact, and its direct consequences, will eventually be "turned into rebirth," the state described in the paragraph above.

"The divine spirit" is the same as the Supreme Being, or rather the portion of It specific human beings will be able to "access," so to say, which will be much more stupendous experience than we can currently imagine. Of course the humans will rejoice. They will be ecstatic, as they, once again, will be able to merge with the Word, the ancient Logos, and "hear" from It all the knowledge and wisdom they need.

> "The divine word will give the substance a gift
> containing heaven and earth, occult gold in the mystic deed,
> all powerful body, soul, spirit.
> Everything is at his feet as if upon a heavenly seat." 3/2

The "substance" are the human beings. Otherwise the quatrain 3/2 more or less rephrases and reconfirms what was said in quatrain 2/13. The "gift" is the knowledge of everything that was, is, and will be, on this Earth, in the entire Universe. The "occult gold" though refers to a fabled alchemical purification process that consisted of seven stages, resulting in the production of gold. However, this alchemical idea was also borrowed from, and confused with, the idea of the "purification" of human species, we call here the Guided Evolution. It was destined, as all the major mythological systems were aware of, to go through six stages, of which this happens to be the sixth one, before human beings are, in the seventh stage, transformed into "golden beings," or divine beings, after which no more refinements will be needed. The words "mystic deed" most likely refers to the entire process of the purification of mankind and its final deliverance; a process still all too mysterious at this stage.

The reacquired divinity, that will recombine "body, spirit, soul" in every human being, will indeed produce an "all powerful" new species, as was already explained, able to perceive of everything, including the micro-world and macro-world, from the Supreme Being's perspective, the named otherworldly "heavenly seat."

Yet, while all of these fabulous predictions will be fulfilled, our deliverance will take place barely at the very last moment. Most likely in order to make us think about all the "coincidences."

> "When the lamp burning with eternal fire
> will be found in the temple of Vestals,
> a child found (in the) fire(water) passing through the sieve ..." 9/9

While the above (portion of the) quatrain closely echoes a Persian myth of Apam Napat, it also manages to compile a symbolic image upon a symbolic image.

Where, historically, the Vestals are long gone, the eternal fire they were symbolically guarding in their temples is still burning. It is the flickering fire of the human spirit, embodied in the "child," that is the immature mankind. In turn this "child" is about to leave the eternal fire(water) that still sustains it, and float out "through the sieve" of evolution into oblivion, but will be saved in the last moment. I should add here that, while you can imagine the fire-water, (or burning alcohol), to represent the human spirit, in the ancient ceremonies fires used to be built near pools of water to reflect in them at night, and this reflection symbolized the spiritual "fire" emanating symbolically from the polar glaciers, floating on water. If it needs further clarification, I would add that, most likely, without the Supreme Being's interference, the polar glaciers would melt completely, and our minds would be virtually snuffed out. As a consequence, we would end up being worse off than animals. At that stage, we would hardly be able to learn from our past mistakes, and the entire process of Guided Evolution could come to a screeching halt. Worse yet, within a few thousand years, as our solar system will leave the protective space bubble, life on this planet would be obliterated by numerous impacting asteroids, if we were not around and able to prevent that.

> "The end of the wolf, the lion, ox & the ass,
> the timid deer will be with the mastiffs.
> No longer will the sweet manna fall upon them —
> more vigilance & custody for the mastiffs." 10/99

The individual animals represent the totem clans of the Bear Cult, headed nominally by Artemis. (In countries that had no bears, or in which the connection to the Bear Cult had to be eventually hidden, out of fear of religious persecution, a lion, even a crocodile, were used as substitutes.) There will be no need for these totem clans in the future, because there will be no need for the Bear Cult. There will be no need of it, because the planet will no longer fall into decay, following major climatic changes, and people will no longer lapse into savagery and ignorance, following such events; a situation out of which they were being periodically extricated by the Bear Cult.

The "deer," in mythological terms, represents the spirit, and the Latin word "dama," (i.e. deer), used by Nostradamus in the original, also means in many European languages the "lady," which in turn points to Mother Earth, and her various defense aspects. Yet, in the future, this defense aspect will have to become a conscious part of mankind's behaviour, implemented with foresight, and carried out by human guardians Nostradamus calls "the mastiffs," a breed of large, powerful dogs. It would be only fitting to point out that, in ancient times, dogs used to be considered the guardians of sacred knowledge. This knowledge, in turn, is intimately tied to our Guided Evolution, and to its goal.

It will be these "mastiffs" who will be responsible for the fate of the planet and of all the life here, including the human one, because beyond this stage, the Supreme Being, by the nature of our future predicaments, will no longer be able to help us, which is what the line "No longer will the sweet manna fall upon them" is saying. Soon, the human evolution will be deemed completed, and we shall become fully responsible for any action we take, or fail to take.

TIME CYCLES & CONVERGING PROPHECIES

We take the concept of linear time, introduced in the Bible, for granted, especially since it is intimately linked in our minds with the current concept of history, Darwinian dogma, and the general idea of "progress marching irreversibly forward." Yet, all such ideas are, aside from the aforementioned Bible, of fairly recent vintage, because until the 17th century, a cyclical concept of time was the norm in Europe, and till much more recently, among the more "primitive" cultures of the world. In fact most people in India remain firm believers in the principle of the cyclical nature of time till this day.

Without a doubt, for Nostradamus, the concept of cyclical time was also the norm, because he was likely aware of the fact that ALL the known time cycles will be converging during the 20th and the 21st centuries, about 500 years from the time he recorded his predictions. As he stated in quatrain 3/79: "The fatal and eternal order of the cycle will turn in due order."

This "cycle" though consists of several sub-cycles. The shortest of these, interestingly enough, is about 500 years long. It separates the emergence of dominant cultures within the pre-existent formative civilizations. This phenomenon was known since the prehistoric times, and the ancient Egyptians used to refer to it as "the rising of the Phoenix from its ashes."

Their story of it is rather convoluted and confused, like most Egyptian "myths." It speaks of two "birds," the "papa bird," and the "son bird." The son bird brings the "dead" body of his "father" from abroad, somewhere, wrapped in a flammable cocoon that bursts into flames, out of which the "new" Phoenix is (re)born.

While the Egyptians were "masters" of muddling up every abstract idea they inherited, or simply just stumbled on, somehow, they usually managed to retain a kernel of truth in whatever they preserved. In this instance, they even managed to preserve for us a bit of ambiguity, surrounding the figure of 500 years, claiming it was sometimes closer to 400 years, sometimes to 600 years.

Indeed, having pored over the many dates associated with the rise and fall of individual cultures, or distinct stages within major civilizations, I can concur the 500 year long period is merely an agreed on average, and that there is nothing precisely mechanical about it. After all, nature is not a machine.

For example, within the context of Western civilization, 16th century definitely represents a departure from the dominance of the Catholic Church culture, and the emergence of the new mercantilistic / scientific system. The 500 years preceding the ascend of the Catholic Church culture, roughly from 11th century on, was devoted to the establishing of the current European nations, with the help of the "budding" Church. The Roman Empire also lasted some 500 years, until its division into the eastern part, Byzantium, and its struggling western part, or about 600 years, till the complete defeat and collapse of the western part. The 500 years before Rome belong to classical Greece, and the preceding few centuries, we can say, were all a part of the original molding of the coming Western civilization in general, with ideas borrowed from the preceding formative civilization.

In turn each formative civilization is allocated a period of about 3,000 years—more or less the time elapsed from the "inception" of the European civilization. The preceding 3,000 year long cycle started some 6,000 years ago in Sumer, (4,000 B.C.E.), from where it later influenced the formation of civilization in Egypt.

The awareness of this particular cycle was preserved for us in China and Greece. The Chinese mythological sources speak of the "peaches of immortality," that grew in the Western Paradise, home of Hsi Wang Mu, the Queen Mother of the West. According to this tradition, the magical peach trees first flower for 3,000 years, and the next 3,000 years the peaches ripen. More people though will be familiar with the golden apples that grew in the Garden of the Hesperides. It was the task of the Greek cultural hero, Hercules, to bring those apples from the said Garden, located, again, somewhere in the west. Most researchers into that subject agree it was located in the north-western part of the Sahara. But what today is an inhospitable desert, used to be a fertile, forested, and well watered country, where a fairly advanced culture with roads, chariots, large cities and amphitheatres was flourishing, until about 5,000 to 6,000 years ago. It was that very culture that was represented by the golden apples. The reason for this particular symbology was at least twofold: 1) Gold refers to the fabled Golden Age. 2) Apples were believed to carry souls from one body to the next. The combined message suggests a transmission of the "soul," or "spirit" of the Golden Age to the succeeding formative civilizations.

In the connection with the 3,000 year long cycles we should also mention the conviction of the Pythagoreans, who claimed it takes 3,000 years for a soul to mature through various "reincarnations." More likely than not, it was the "reincarnations" of the individual cultures within the formative civilization that gave rise to this idea, whose original concept was beyond the Greeks' comprehension, by then. Incidentally, there were four Hesperid "sisters" in the Garden. Assuming that each one of them represents "one apple," we would end up with a period of 12,000 years, the Age of the Moon, or the entire period of spiritual / mental darkness, that the ancients knew was coming. And this is no haphazard conclusion, because the classical Greek literature, for example the Homeric epic poems, are filled with such symbols.

In either case, the 12,000 year long period obviously represents another such cycle, also introduced by Nostradamus, the awareness of which was recorded for us in various other ways by the ancient cultures. For example, the Persian lore, focused on the god of light Ahura Mazda, claims that he will regain supremacy, and defeat the "evil" Ahriman, in 12,000 years. Intriguingly enough, the predictions surrounding the circumstances of his return include the following details: The end will arrive in three stages: 1. Peace and generosity are introduced, followed by a disaster in form of torrential rain. 2. A subsequent cycle of peace and prosperity is followed by a tyranny. 3. The final transformation arrives.

Unfortunately, the more complex mythologized messages have been, more often than not, usually tempered with. For example, by reversing the order of events, which is the case here, where the stages 1 & 2 have been flipped. Then the original stage 1 will correspond to the pre-World War I situation, followed by the tyrannies of the communist and fascist ilk. The stage 2 will correspond to the post-World War II situation, and the arrival of the greenhouse effect, its initial stages marked by torrential rains and floods some places, (re: Nostradamus' predictions for Persia after the asteroid's impact), and draughts in others. Stage 3 remains the same: final transformation.

Having just reread the Egyptian sacred "*Book of That Which is in the Underground*," that describes Ra's (that is the Sun's) voyage through the twelve hours of darkness, I am now certain this book is also about the 12,000 years of mental / spiritual darkness on Earth.

Using one set of imagery, the 12,000 year long period of the Moon Age can be divided up into four periods of 3,000 years each, or two complete "seasons" of cultural flowering and of cultural fruits. On the other hand, in the Indian tradition, the same 12,000 years represent one complete cycle of Mahayuga, or Great Cycle, which in turn is composed of four sub-cycles of unequal duration, and of progressively worsening conditions. The first of these sub-cycles is known as Krta Yuga, and lasts 4,800 years. The next one is Treta Yuga, which is composed of 3,600 years. Then comes Davarapa Yuga, of 2,400 years, and finally the Kali Yuga, which lasts 1,200 years—and we happen to be living right now through the last few decades of its duration, which are to end in a "dissolution."

Kali Yuga is usually described as "the age of darkness." Yet, it too has its redeeming values, without which the people could not go on living. For example, if we were to inquire about the root causes of the current disintegration of the society, of family, of spiritual, and even of "plain" human values, we would have to realize they are all connected to our misconstrued concept of freedom, recombined with egoism, greed, exploitation and alienation. "In the Indian view, every man of the Kali Yuga is stimulated to seek his freedom," notes Mircea Eliade in "*The Myth of the Eternal Return.*"

The name of this cycle is inseparable from the goddess Kali, after whom it is named. She is usually viewed as a goddess of death and destruction, wreaked on a massive scale. But it is only one aspect of this dualistic "goddess," who is also, and mainly, known as Shakti, the "Power," that is the motive power of the (human) "gods," without which they would be, and presently are, completely powerless. In this positive aspect, she also represents the generative (and regenerative) power of the world at large. Simply put, Kali is the punitive aspect of Shakti, just like Artemis is the punitive aspect of Gaia, and once the Age of Kali is over, the Age of Shakti will return.

Nominally, the god Shiva is designated as Kali's "husband." But while he is usually portrayed "dead," to illustrate the absence of the Shakti's aspect, he is, at the same time, portrayed with an oversized erect penis—which 'hints' at the presence of promiscuity and overpopulation during such a cycle.

The 12,000 year long period is also mentioned, in a "veiled" fashion, by the playwright Aeschylus, an initiate of the Eleusinian mysteries, and as such familiar with these topics, in his play *Prometheus Bound*. Towards the end of this play the goddess Io, cursed by Hera and transformed into a cow, whose horns also designate her as a Moon goddess, appears on the scene, where she has the following exchange with the newly chained Prometheus.

> Prometheus— I shall be freed by one of your offsprings.
> Io— What do you mean? You freed by a child of mine!
> Prometheus— After twelve generations have passed away.
> Io— Ah, you veil your language now, like the oracles.

The last two sentences make it quite obvious that no ordinary human generations were meant, nor of the Olympian gods, who were nominally immortal. This "veiled" reference was intended for the trained ears of the initiates of the Eleusinian mysteries, who numbered in the tens of thousands in ancient Greece, and who understood the figure to be twelve millennia. After all, in the same play Prometheus earlier states: "I must strive through thousands of years, strive on to the goal."

We find a couple of such "veiled" references even in the closing scenes of Homer's Illiad. When Odysseus finally returns to Ithaca, he first goes by a "nearby mill," inhabited by twelve women. Eleven of them are "asleep," only the youngest one is "milling," while praying to Zeus to stop the feasting in the halls of Odysseus, which is plundering the land. A day later the hero returns to his palace as a beggar, (re: the poor shall inherit the land), and wins the contest for his own wife by shooting an arrow through twelve axes.

Symbolism of this sort abounds on the pages of the Homeric

texts, including the *Illiad*. To start with the twelve axes, we can quite safely say they represent twelve "generations," i.e. millennia, of plunder of this planet, and the "gods" of those time periods. Odysseus wife and estate then represent the planet. The "mill" women could also represent the same 12,000 year cycle, which would make Odysseus a vengeful "Kali," and he does behave like one, slaughtering all the "guests," with the exception of the bard, who is under the protection of the gods. But, equally likely, if not more so, the "mill" represents the "God's mill" of the Zodiac, an idea explored with magisterial sweep in *Hamlet's Mill*, by Hertha von Dechend and Giorgio de Santillana, which brings us to the subject of the longest cycle we know of. Concerning its division, discussions flare up occasionally among astrologers whether we are still in the Age of Pisces, or whether we have already passed into the Age of Aquarius. Considering all the other influences, and considering that no detectable line can exist in time, separating these two ages, or any of the other cycles, such discussions are pointless and ridiculous. Nostradamus was likely well aware of the fact, which is why he spoke of "Jupiter returning," referring to the influence of the passing cycle.

For example, the same way the Indians add 10 percent for the "dawn," and 10 percent for the "dusk" of each Yuga cycle, we have to do the same with each Zodiac sign. Since they are about 2,150 years long, we ought to consider a transition period of about 200 years on each side of each Zodiac sign, before the corresponding conditions establish themselves or, on the other hand, cease influencing the new conditions. And taking into consideration several ancient indicators, I am inclined to believe that the Age of Aquarius nominally started some 50 years ago, but it is going to take another 50 years, or so, before the people will start to feel its presence. Furthermore, the New Age interpreters are talking only about the implied simplicity of this age, while completely ignoring that the very symbol of Aquarius spells out the coming of a dreadful global flood.

Most important of all though is the fact that, in a very near future, the influences of ALL the six named cycles are going to overlap—with shattering results for all the current societies. And, as we have noted, it is precisely this period of "overlap" that most of Nostradamus' key predictions focus on. To underline the crucial importance of this period, we should note, again, that during the end of the previous Zodiac cycle, some 25,800 years ago, the civilization incinerated itself. In fact, the entire planet was in flames, as myths from several diverse sources confirm. This conflict then resulted in a "nuclear winter."

This mind-bending concept of time cycles, along with the concept of Jovian and Saturnian 'cultural' cycles, also "suggest" eons long periods of careful observations and records, upon which the reality of these cycles was founded and which we know nothing about. By the same token, we know nothing either of the five preceding cycles of civilizations, responsible for these findings, which makes our concept of reality substantially flawed.

But before we can part company with this chapter though, we still have to examine a few representative samples of ancient prophecies, all converging on our times.

Although erroneously interpreted as arriving during the lifetimes of Jesus and his followers, some of these prophecies, hoary with time, wound up in the New Testament, borrowed, at least in part, from various Hebrew prophets. They include the arrival and impact of the asteroid, massive destruction and loss of human life, as well as the coming of "the Kingdom of God," and "deification" of mankind.

"… the sign of the Son of Man will appear in the sky …" (Mat 24-30) "great star falls from heaven, burning like a torch … something like a giant mountain was thrown in the sea …" (Rev 8-10, 8) Thus describes St. John, who, some suspect, was Jesus himself, 'his vision' of this future event, rendered in the past tense. "But immediately after the tribulation of those days the sun will be darkened, and the moon will not give its light, the stars," i.e. the fiery fragments, "will fall from the sky …" (Mat 24-29) The prophet Isaiah contributed these two details: "There shall be strict darkness without dawn … for there comes a smoke from the north." (14-25, 31) And during these events "… two men in the field, one will be taken, one left." (Mat 24-40) A passage in the Revelation suggests the remaining half will be further reduced by wars and plagues.

Yet, while the situation will be desperate, and genuinely tragic, it will not be hopeless, for "The Son of Man has come to save that which has been lost." (Mat 18-11) That is the human mental / spiritual qualities. "… for the sake of the elect these days shall be cut short." (Mat 24-22)

Although it will be difficult for the orthodox believers to accept that Jesus will "come back" as an asteroid, they have to keep in mind that the authors of the Bible were all too preoccupied with parables, especially Jesus himself, because the ordinary folks would not have understood the straight facts. More likely than not, even Jesus' and Matthew's understanding of such matters was, at best, third hand, and thus severely limited. Yet, they knew that, in the end, "the righteous will shine forth as the sun in the Kingdom of their Father," (Mat 13-43), and that people will, in effect, be like gods. That was simply their way of saying that the Age of the Sun will return.

The Nordic Ragnarorok offers virtually identical prediction of the same critical period: "The sun will darken // land will drown in sea // into the depth are falling // burning stars." This one sentence essentially encapsulates chapters The Asteroid Impact and The Flood.

According to the Indian lore, the future tenth incarnation of Vishnu, an avatar Kalki, will be "a beautiful lad sitting on a white horse, with a sword like a meteor, spreading death and destruction." Yet, "his arrival is again going to restore justice on Earth, bring back the age of purity and innocence." Or, as another version says, "renew the dignity … (the) life goals." Furthermore, this Kalki was expected to arrive "at the end of the dark age, when casts," i.e. values, "will become confused, when thieves without character will proliferate … (when) under the guise of religion, irreligiosity will be proclaimed." (From *Agni Purana.)*

Even the Roman poet Virgil offers a vision of our near future, in his *Bucolica* (IV): "The last age has risen, as the Cumaen prophecy foretold; The great order of ages is beginning anew, yet again the Virgin is returning, and the Saturnian empire is coming back, a new human race is already being sent by high heaven. Protect the boy who is supposed to come, shy Lucy, your brother now already reigns: with him is ending the iron race, but the golden one shall arise all over the world. Then, when you are of age, and reach maturity, the trader will leave the sea on his own, the goods will not be loaded and unloaded, because every region will produce everything."

Here we have to pause and interpret as best as possible. 1) The last age refers to the Age of Pisces. 2) The prophecy was transmitted to the public by the Sybil priestesses, residing in the sacred cave of Cumae, near Naples, who were dedicated to the Triple Hecate. 3) The Virgin is either Artemis, or simply the renewed inviolability of Nature, symbolically deemed perennially "virginal." 4) Lucy is Juno Lucina, goddess of Celestial Light—most likely a version of Shakti, the Universal Spirit. 5) The "boy" most likely is the "child" now about to "pass through the sieve," of quatrain 9/9, or rather the immature mankind about to be reborn. 6) Her "brother" was known as Genious, or the "male spirit." His departure also seems to be suggesting a decline of patriarchy, most likely to be replaced by a (hopefully) modified form of matriarchy. 7) We should also note here that, while Juno Lucina's consort was, in the past, Jupiter, Virgil was talking about the return of "the Saturnian empire," long before the New Testament spoke of the coming Kingdom of God. 8) The "iron race" represents our civilization, unthinkable without iron and other metals, but the expression also refers to the Iron Age in general. 10) The reference to the demise of the mercantilists echoes the prediction transmitted by Nostradamus—but also by the prophet Isaiah.

However, since most of the trade within the Babylonian empire, which Isaiah was familiar with, was conducted from river boats, he adjusted his prediction accordingly: "In a place of rivers and wide streams, on which no boat is rowed, where no majestic ship passes …" (Isaiah 33-21) The same prediction is also referred to in Homer's *Illiad*, as Ulysses also gives up his sea trading.

The Chinese, who recognize four ancient dynasties, namely the Yellow, (re: gold) symbolized by earth, the Green, symbolized by wood, the White, symbolized by metal, and the Red, symbolized by fire, also speak of a future "dynasty," whose color is Black, and which is symbolized by water—i.e. the global flood. Then a new "dynasty" of earth (i.e. of gold) will arise, we are told by this lore.

Even the various other hints of timing, scattered as they are, point to our time period. A mythological Persian ruler named Kai Kusrau allegedly proclaimed ages ago: "The whole world is my kingdom … from Pisces … to the Bull's head … from today new feasts and customs date." As should be obvious, Kai Kusrau was counting backwards, from "our" Age of Pisces to "his" Age of Taurus, a time span of some 6,500 years, representing the darkest period of recent human history. What remains unsaid in this brief quote is that after the Age of Pisces is over, a yet another system of "feasts and customs" will be dated.

By far the most striking are the dated prophecies of this coming transformation. Nostradamus, while not quite certain of the dating, selected July 1999. The Babylonian high priest and astronomer / astrologer, named Berossus, offered a date corresponding to May 5,

2000. The Mayans predicted the end of this cycle would arrive by, or on, December 21st, 2012. And so far, admittedly, the timing of their predictions is the most accurate of any people. In either case though, in spite of their origins, so distant in place and time, all these dates are incredibly close to each other.

It is certainly also worth mentioning that the famous Swiss psychoanalyst Carl Gustav Jung, shortly before his death in 1961, had a series of visions of a future great catastrophe of fiery nature, taking place in about fifty years time, according to Marie-Louise von Franz, the custodian of Jung's personal notes. While most people who came to know of them proposed the idea of a nuclear war to explain these visions, I would opt for the arrival of the asteroid.

Glancing back now over this compilation of quotes from sources whose origin is really diverse, both in place and time, we can see they all agree on the basic facts, including the timing.

AFTERWORD

The contents of the preceding chapters can be summed up, as was promised, in a few sentences: Unexpectedly, an asteroid will appear, and within a few days will impact the Earth. This impact will be the cause of dreadful tidal waves, of the steep rise of the sea level, and of the subsequent "asteroid winter." These consequences will deprive people of living space and serve as causes for decades of brutal wars of extermination. At the same time the changed planetary conditions of the new ice age will, within a generation or two, dramatically improve and transform the mental / spiritual capacity of mankind, turning people into demigods. In the process the people will realize as well that there indeed is a transcendent Supreme Being, and that it was this Being who created the Universe, actually became the Universe and all the Life within It, and has guided our evolution, to make our species worthy of the role we are expected to fulfill—to protect and enhance the Life on this planet.

Snippets of this knowledge, scattered all over the world, have existed for long millennia within various mythological systems. There is no doubt in my mind that some of the biblical prophets, as well as the Essenians, of whom Jesus was one, also became acquainted with such a brief outline of the future, at least to a certain degree. However, they lacked a key piece of information. Namely, they did not know when these events will occur. This not only led to quarrels among the prophets, but it also led Jesus to promise his disciples this transformation will come during their lifetimes. As we all know by now, that promise was about 2,000 years premature.

Ultimately, the only proof a prophecy can have is its fulfillment. Yet, the core of Nostradamus' prophecies would have remained unforetold—if not properly interpreted, and if that interpretation, as provided in this book, did not come true. Also, as already noted, more than once, Nostradamus 'merely' updated a collection of very ancient predictions, and by "scrambling" them, he achieved the desirable goal: making them notoriously known for centuries to come—in order to reach their interpreter.

And no, it is not vanity speaking here, because Nostradamus has foretold quite a few details about the personality of this interpreter, and his circumstances, where these are connected to the book itself, in four, perhaps five quatrains. Two of them are so personal, only the indicated individual would be able to understand the references contained in them.

> "For five hundred more years they will hold in esteem
> the one who was the ornament of his age:
> A great empowering stroke of clarity is granted,
> which will make the people of that century very content." 3/94

These words were written over 450 years ago, and they too will be fulfilled, because Nostradamus is certainly going to remain famous for at least the next 50 years. At the same time this quatrain also helps to date the period during which the "great empowering stroke of clarity (will be) granted," or at least made public. That period is now—just before the impact of the asteroid, and the subsequent events. To deliver the correct interpretation after the fact would be pointless. Obviously, it will not be the prediction of the impact, nor of its consequences, "which will make the people of (this) century very content," but the predictions of the much later events, including the deification of mankind. However, people will be made equally content by the proof of the Supreme Being's existence, of Its involvement in our affairs. Furthermore, it is this proof that lies at the heart of all prophecies. These certainly do not exist for their sake, as tools of personal or national glorification, at least not the genuine ones, but were intended solely as basis for such a future proof. In turn the "transmitters," i.e. Nostradamus and other such prophets, as well as this "interpreter," are only mere instruments of the stated purpose. (By the same token, one can realize only in retrospect to have been selected, somehow, to be such an instrument.)

"The Moon in the vastness of the night over the high mountain.
A man of new wisdom, his unaided mind has seen it.
Summoned by his disciples to become immortal,
eyes looking south, writing in his heart, body on fire." 4/31

This quatrain, more than anything else, reminds me of an abstract painting two of my former friends were joking over, being intimately familiar with the subject, which was a party they both attended, and since one was the author of it.

It would be only appropriate to point out that I have read this quatrain many times previously, without making the assumption that it was about me, until I have almost finished this book. Only then it started to make sense.

Here the Moon not only stands for the light reflected off the spiritual Sun, shining in the vast deep night of our present times, but I was also born, in the astrological sense, under the sign of the Moon. Furthermore, my surname in English, or French, would be Montane, or mountaineer, a man from the mountains. Since I am over six feet tall, one could also say that I am a "high mountain," illuminated by the light of the Moon. Yet, with the Moon being my birth sign, the suggestion could also be made that I am "self-illuminated."

The "new wisdom" is presented in this book only partially. More of it can be found in the other books I wrote. The reader should also keep in mind that much of this "new wisdom" is actually very, very ancient wisdom, this author was able to glean from myths, with some help from modern sciences, using only his "unaided mind," because no one else was either able or willing to see it there before, and thus "aid" my mind.

The last line, as far as my inner biography is concerned, is the most intriguing one, because all the related ideas I have developed only started to come into focus after my "eyes looking south" glimpsed the key interconnecting piece of the labyrinthine puzzle of our existence. The word "south," in this case, refers to the South Pole, or more generally, to the Antarctic.

About thirty years ago some astrophysicists came up with a theory that intelligent life evolved within only about 0.6 percent of solar systems. From elsewhere I remembered that the human brain represents about 0.6 percent of the average body weight. Then, some twenty five years ago, I came across the figure of 0.6 percent again. It referred to the amount of planetary water found in form of ice—and most of it located in the Antarctic.

Since I have already made a connection between the two previously identified "sacred" numbers (of 0.6 percent), I accepted this figure as a part of a "sacred triad." Then, with consternation, I asked myself: What would happen to the intelligence of the human species, which is presently not very great to start with, if all the polar and other glaciers were to melt during the expected planetary warm up?! My subsequent research convinced me that it too would melt, even further, just as it did melt away in the period between 11,700 and 10,200 years ago, when the Antarctic was largely free of glaciers, and the Arctic completely so, with the exception of Greenland.

Always wanting to be a writer, not just a poet, I have been searching, till that moment, for a theme, subject, to devote my writing life to. From then on though, I did indeed have "writing in my heart," because I was doing something that really mattered. Equally true is the statement about the "body on fire," at least figuratively speaking, since my metabolism was in a high gear for decades, which always made me exceptionally thirsty, as if in a need to quench an inner fire. Nowadays, this "fire" rises fairly often to a fever pitch, albeit mainly due to health reasons.

Admittedly, I know of no disciples at this stage, neither of summons to immortality, but only of a solitary task I carry on with, because I simply feel the urge, the obsession to do so, strengthened now by the suggestion of rare predestination.

> "The one before the last of the prophet's surname
> will take Artemis for his light & repose.
> Wandering far in his frenetic test,
> delivering great people from deception." 2/28

The prophet is generally assumed to be Mohammed, rendered as Mahomet, during Nostradamus' times. (Re: 5/55) "The one before the last of the prophet's surname" then is "ho," as in the author's surname: Horak. This could be nothing more but a wild presumption, and for a while it was, if it did not correlate so closely with quatrain 4/31. When I first saw this reference, I admit I knew next to nothing about Artemis, but I diligently started to rectify that omission. And indeed, the study of Artemis' role illuminated for me a large portion of the puzzles coded into myths. In this respect Artemis did become my guiding light. By now I view this quatrain as a reminder sign, posted for me by Nostradamus, and endlessly wonder how he had received his instruction for doing so.

Regarding the third line, I can say that, as a young person, I was, most likely incorrectly, diagnosed with jaundice. Being discharged from the hospital, I was told not to do any hard work, and to completely avoid alcohol, for a period of one year, minimum. But while recovering, at our acquaintances' country farm, combined with a pub, I decided to test my fate. I went with the adult guys to the forest, where I was heaving pieces of yard long cordwood onto a truck. Upon returning, I went to the liquor alcove, poured myself a shot from each bottle there, and then proceeded to the cherry orchard, to lay down under a tree, awaiting the results. Since my liver did not turn into stone, I surmised, however childishly, that I was meant to live, to accomplish something important. Still, this "experiment" did not take place on a spur of the moment, but followed three close brushes with death.

Years later, I left my native country, Czechoslovakia, in search of knowledge, unshackled not only by the communist censorship, but by any dogma what-so-ever. Enrolling eventually at a university, I realized scholastic dogma thrives everywhere, and decided to pursue knowledge on my own. To facilitate the process, I started a small publishing company, which generally left me plenty of time for reading. The subjects included mainly history, sociology, ecology, philosophy, various branches of science, anthropology, mythologies, as well as some poetry and literature. I also traveled all over Europe and North America, including Mexico, in order to see as much as possible, as a part of my search for knowledge.

It is my sincere hope that this, and the other books in the series, will indeed "deliver great people from deception." The "great people," of course, are the inhabitants of the North American continent, the future formative civilization of the world. The "deception" is the mental construct of the society, forced upon us by the current plutocratic / scientific establishment.

> "False topography will be exposed,
> the urns of the hidden monuments revealed.
> The sect of holy philosophy will thrive —
> black for white & the new for the old." 7/14

The term "false topography" is a virtual synonym for the term "deception," from the preceding quatrain 2/28. The "hidden monuments" are the glorious mental structures of the hoary past, now "hidden," buried in "the urns" of the tragedy of human forgetfulness. This book is, I trust, but the first installment of this "holy philosophy," around which such a "sect" will form, in due time, and then it "will thrive" in the near future. The last line tells us that what now formally masquerades as the "good," or white (magic, we could say), for example the big business, will turn out to be "black," or evil (magic). In a more straightforward fashion, the old life-destroying system will be replaced by a new, life-affirming one, with the help of this philosophy.

> "A man will be charged with the destruction
> of temples & sects, altered by fantasy,
> He will harm the stones rather than the living,
> filling ears with ornate speeches." 1/96

It will be the "ornate speeches," appropriately embellished with knowledge, addressing congregations, which will cause "the destruction of temples and sects," rather than a brute force. The "sects altered by fantasy" are all the main current religious orders, as well as the groups worshiping Mammon. Most likely the new "holy philosophy" will be the source of inspiration for these "ornate speeches," presented by many of its male and female adherents, when the time will come.

> "The lost thing found, hidden for a long cycle (of time).
> The Pastor will be honoured as a demigod,
> when the moon completes her great cycle,
> but by other rumors he shall be dishonoured." 1/25

All the interpretations I know of attribute this quatrain to Luis Pasteur, and his discovery of germs, their fatal role during surgeries. Yet, during Pasteur's time, which was most of the 19th century, the Moon Age was still at least 150 years from the completion of its cycle. Thus it could hardly have been him, in spite the fact he was indeed acknowledged as a demigod during his lifetime. If this quatrain refers to this author as the "pastor," or "shepherd" of a future "flock," or simply as a person promoting "pastoral" values, he will most likely not be thus honoured until "the moon completes her great cycle," starting more than 20 years in the future, by which time he will hardly be among the living, and hardly be in the position to either defend himself, or to care about any rumors.

However, the last line contains two other possibilities of

interpretation: 1) People won't be exactly angelic even at the onset of the Age of the Sun. 2) Such a dating is in itself quite uncertain, because the Age of the Sun is technically upon us already—but it will reverse itself after the asteroid's impact, according to Nostradamus. In this case, he might be referring to the present. If that were so, then the many people whose concept of reality will crumble, or whose base of power will be threatened, will understandably lash out against such philosophy and its author. That, one way or the other, is inevitable anyhow.

With this concludes the re-examination of Nostradamus' quatrains. I hope you found it a rewarding, if not an easy reading. It was never meant as a titillating past-time, but as a "life-vest" for those who are willing and capable of grasping it. I trust you are.